How *Not* To Cry

A Guide to Emotional Freedom for Sensitive People

Steph Dodds

GRATITUDE
HOUSE
PUBLISHING

Gratitude House Publishing

Sacramento, California

How Not To Cry: A Guide to Emotional Freedom for Sensitive People
1. Self Help 2. Spirituality 3. Personal Growth

Hardcover ISBN 979-8-9863887-2-4

Tradepaper ISBN 979-8-9863887-0-0

Ebook ISBN 979-8-9863887-1-7

Author Photos by Carley Stephens

Cover and interior photos by Carley Stephens

Worksheets created by Steph Dodds

Edited by Nora-Joanne Gerber, Cynthia Gregory, and Emma Moylan

Cover and Interior Book Design by Lilly Penhall

The names of people in this book have been changed for privacy.

First edition September 2022

Printed in the United States of America.

Contents

PREPARING THE SOIL..ix
Introduction xi
1: Being Sensitive 1
2: An Introduction to Emotional Freedom Techniques............11
3: Principles of the Process..23
4: Emotional Wellbeing & Maintenance 35

SEEDING 49
5: Health & the Physical Body..51
6: Weight Loss 65
7: Addiction 79
8: Self-Love & Acceptance 89
9: Relationships..103
10: Prosperity & Abundance 119
11: Achievements & Goals 131
12: Creativity, Flow, and Going for Your Dreams...................141

THE HARVEST 153
13: Self-Guided Tapping & Working with Limiting Beliefs 155
14: Tapping with Kids, Pets and Groups...............................169
15: More Tools For Taking Care Of Your Energy 179

Conclusion 191
Resources 195
Acknowledgments 197
About the Author...199

This book is dedicated to your future self.
And to all your future selves who are feeling lighter,
clearer, and more emotionally free.
May your future YOU be looking back on you,
smiling with gratitude.

*eventually you start to see changes.
your mind becomes light, the trees look
bright, the air you breathe begins to feel
like food for new opportunity, and life
takes on a crisp color pattern. ups and
downs will continue to come and there is
still much to learn, but you are calm now
and do not fear the old storms, which seem
to pass more quickly. a new awareness arises
to gently remind you that your power is
yours to wield and is ready to propel you
forward into peace and liberating insight.*

yung pueblo

PREPARING THE SOIL

Introduction

"I understand now that I'm not a mess but a deeply feeling person in a messy world. I explain that now, when someone asks me why I cry so often, I say, 'For the same reason I laugh so often—because I am paying attention.'"

—Glennon Doyle

Welcome to my world. You may have picked up this book because you can relate to the *How Not to Cry* title or have a loved one who may experience some of the struggles that come with being a sensitive person. Perhaps you have had a hard time in this wild world because due to your sensitivity, you have picked up on everyone else's energy, felt emotions much more deeply than the other people around you, and felt *FOR* the other people around you. Perhaps you have a *sensitive cryer type* in your life, and you would like to learn more about how to help and better understand them. As I see it, this book is not just for people who cry a lot. If you are a coach, a healer, a teacher, or a therapist, you are bound to run into sensitive people, and this book holds a great gift that everyone can use to move through the twists and turns of this human experience.

I have always been a highly sensitive person, and it has always been incredibly embarrassing. A stigma can follow us *sensitive cryer types* around: that we are weird, easily overwhelmed, weak, or just simply "too much." I never quite felt like I was cut out for thriving in today's world. If I am honest, I felt shame for feeling so fiercely, loving, and hurting so deeply, and I was pretty sure there was something wrong with me. Why can't I have it "together" like (*seemingly*) everyone else? Not feeling *EVERYTHING* kind of seems like living a good life, impartial, indifferent, a whatever-easy-breezy kind of life.

I know that old familiar sensation of not wanting to speak, as I knew the moment I would open my mouth for words to come out is when all of the emotions would accompany them. My face would feel hot, my palms clammy, and the tidal wave of emotion would wash over me, or more like, burst out of me. There was no conscious decision in the matter; it just happened. I have honestly fantasized about having the option to cry or not to cry. A friend of mine from college told me once, "Steph, it is not that I am shallow; you are just really deep."

I now believe our tears are actually an incredible gift. They are a sign of strength. I will go as far as suggesting that having tears is a privilege, as not everyone has access to that deep level of feeling. As a sensitive person, you have an opportunity to feel, the opportunity to let stuff go instead of stuff it down, and the opportunity for spiritual guidance from a higher realm. What if your emotions actually come up to the surface in order to be released? Maybe it is a good thing, not a bad thing, that "emotional stuff" comes up because it is ready to be liberated and set free. My point is that there is nothing wrong with you, and perhaps there is a more efficient way to channel all of that potent energy you feel for the good of yourself and for all.

The truth is that tears and sensitivity are a superpower, not a villain. In the Buddhist tradition, the teachings tell us that pain is inevitable, but suffering is optional. I want you to know that the real villain here is suffering. I understand that this hyperawareness doesn't feel like a gift for most sensitives, most of the time. I would like to change the language from *sensitive cryer types* in this book together to *emerging superheroes*. Yes, I think you are a superhero. You have a superpower and an incredible gift, but perhaps you do not know how to use this gift efficiently *yet*. Just like when Spider-Man was first learning how to shoot cobwebs from his wrists, it probably did not go smoothly the first time. Imagine if your superpower was shooting laser beams out of your wrists, you might burn down a few buildings before you get the hang of it and hone your skills.

In this book, I will teach you a tool that every *sensitive superhero* should have in their back pocket to move through the emotions of life: EFT (Emotional Freedom Techniques), also known as tapping. Tapping helps us fight off the kryptonite of life (suffering) with a simple tap of the fingertips along with targeted self-talk prompts. EFT tapping helps us move through our emotions in a safe way so that we are not constantly fighting them under the surface. Tapping can help us feel lighter and more present, and guide us into a calm and peaceful place relatively quickly.

There are many books about Emotional Freedom Techniques out there in the world and thank goodness for that. There are many workshops and trainings out there to learn the how-tos for facilitating the structure of this practice. Thank goodness there are dedicated people conducting the clinical trials in order to explain the scientific findings of why EFT can completely change your life in seemingly miraculous ways. If you are interested in the scientific aspect, I highly recommend Dr. Peta Stapleton's book *The Science Behind Tapping*. This book you are holding in your hands is a little different than that, however. It is different because I am speaking to the sensitive types, the empaths, the "criers" and the HSPs (highly sensitive person) of the world who are wondering how we are supposed to navigate through this crazy life being emotionally stable when there are so many factors that can throw us off balance.

When I discovered EFT tapping, I felt a shift within my being immediately. I tapped along as an observer in a live audience, watching Gabby Bernstein do some tapping with a lady on stage. The woman was shaken up from a bicycle accident that day and was still spinning about it. She mentioned how the guy hit her driving very slowly with his car. She did not think she was physically hurt, but was really shaken up about it and starting to feel stiffness in her muscles. The worst part of her experience, she reported, was that she found herself apologizing to him, and trying to shake off the experience on her own. It brought up feelings of always "being in the way" for her and she was apologizing to him for being there and for just existing. Even sitting in the audience, I felt that woman's pain, confusion, and self-doubt. I, of course, teared up a bit. I was plugged into the story, and was tapping along with them in the audience. I had some tears bubbling up on my own, and as we tapped, it felt like some kind of pressure valve was finally releasing inside of me. There was a channel now open, giving a place for all of these feelings to go, and flow. A safe space for the emotions to come up and out of my body.

With the physical touch of the finger tapping and using our words verbally to acknowledge the "problem" or "perceived problem," we are able to release distress from the physical body as well as from mind and spirit. I felt a deep shift; I felt lighter, and even smiled with relief. Even though that may not have been me on the bike, I related to the woman's experience, and had a chance to release some stuck emotions within myself. It was about five minutes of tapping, it wasn't even my issue, and I felt so much better. I knew then and there I needed to learn more about this tapping thing, not knowing at the time that it would end up completely upgrading my life from the inside out, in pretty much every area, and eventually become my profession.

Picture in your mind your ideal backyard garden. Imagine a perfectly manicured victory garden of your dreams. It has your selection of flowers and vegetables growing in it, even a garden gnome or two. For this visualization, imagine something you could easily maintain if you were the sole master gardener of this plot. In World War I and II, folks were encouraged to plant victory gardens to produce their own food and stabilize the country's food supply. Posters encouraged neighbors to "Sow the Seeds of Victory" and have readily available nutrition on hand. As you gaze at your garden on this day, it has been groomed, pruned, and freshly watered. The flowers are bountiful and filled with vibrant color. This piece of land puts off the vibe that it is cherished and has received tender loving care. Imagine this image as a snapshot in time of how one might experience "emotional freedom." Similarly, we will refer to this vision as your emotional freedom garden.

Now imagine this magical garden three weeks later, after not receiving as much attention and keeping. Perhaps there are weeds growing up through the mulch, branches broken and unruly, dried petals and leaves everywhere, wilted sad flowers looking not so vibrant, and maybe some critters have been nibbling at the fruits. Perhaps the wind blew over the birdbath and blew some of the neighbor's trash into your garden.

This wear and tear is a metaphor for plain old life happening. Just as in our emotional garden, day-to-day activities, mishaps, and miscommunication can wear us down. One day we may be feeling on top of the world! And the next day, we may have found out we have ten cavities and require loads of dental work, there is a parking ticket on our windshield, and our favorite pants seem to be too tight.

Life and our emotional well-being require some maintenance and management, and sometimes some good old-fashioned tears. There is no need for shame when our emotional state needs some care either. Emotions are natural and normal. In fact, your emotions have a darn good reason for being there. There is no shame in taking out the trash once a week or brushing our teeth every morning and evening; it is simply maintenance. This is important because there seems to be a social rule that we all need to be OK 100 percent of the time, and grace and patience seem to be missing if we are not. What I am proposing is that there is a better way to feel better, freer, to not fight against yourself anymore. There is no need to make yourself wrong for simply feeling and being alive. You are not alone, you are not too much, and you do have a tribe of people who *FEEL* deeply just like you.

Because of tapping, I am now able to feel and notice my emotions instead of letting them take over my life. I use tapping to get unstuck, so I am better able to use my *sensitivity superpowers* for good. I know how to protect myself from others' energies and clear myself if I need to. As for what to do when a neighbor's trash lands in the garden? I am now able to see that there is nothing wrong with me if this happens, but I am able to take out the metaphorical trash and not take it personally. I can help others now more efficiently instead of being wiped out by other people's energies, opinions, and the ripple effect of their own traumas. I am able to roll up my sleeves and pull out some weeds, attend to my emotional garden any time, and save myself the resentment and grumpiness that comes with things not being well tended to. And I want you to be empowered to do the same thing for yourself.

With tapping, we are able to be with the emotions, acknowledge them, honor them, and let go of excessive emotional charges that are hurting any given situation instead of helping. And when we do this, we have access to our innate wisdom, solutions that may be right in front of us, and a higher perspective that we cannot have access to when we are stuck feeling overwhelmed.

If you are reading this right now, I want you to know that there is hope for you to feel better and that the *suffering part* of feeling life truly is optional. Emotions are normal and natural, and they only become a problem if they get stuck. If we try not to feel what we really feel, that is a recipe for constriction and retraction. Instead of fighting the feelings that come up, tapping is a way to greet the feelings with a welcome sign, a hug, a limo, a cup of freshly brewed organic coffee, and an escort to help get them to where they need to go. We can acknowledge and move through our experiences/feelings/emotions instead of trying not to feel them, only to have them constantly bubble up to the surface over and over again. There is a very practical way to work on your emotional freedom garden for five or ten minutes a day to clear away the natural debris of life, drama, and other people's stuff.

If you are reading this and thinking that feeling your emotions is the last thing you would ever want to do and this feels like an extreme amount of work, I have good news for you. The process I will teach you in this book can even be enjoyable! You would think a book titled *How Not to Cry* would teach you how to stuff things down even more! But it is quite the opposite. Instead of burying those feelings inside for a later time, or for never, or having them manifest as some strange health problem down the road, tapping can help us learn to focus on them, to get to the root of the matter, and release the distress they carry. Accessing that deep root that is invoking the tears is the key to being free of the flowing tears. If we do not do this, they are always lurking right there underneath the surface waiting to strike and causing self-sabotage behaviors. If we take the time to tap and honor the emotions that come up for ourselves, we will no longer need to stuff them down, and therefore have much more energy to thrive and be present for life.

I am excited to introduce you to an effective, quick, self-soothing tool that you can pretty much use anytime and anywhere to keep your emotional freedom garden groomed, pest-free, and thriving. I will teach you how to use this very useful tool of tapping to help you come to a calm and peaceful place within yourself and therefore within the world. This self-help tool can help you honor all of those feelings inside of you, including those that bring tears, so you can move through them as gracefully as possible, and safely let them go, sometimes in a matter of just minutes. EFT is easy to use for yourself once you know how to apply it. Its purpose is to help us let go of repetitive thoughts, negative thinking, emotional distress, and the emotional charge associated with traumatic memories. This can free you up to come back to the present moment, and be your beautiful self again if you happen to get hijacked by an intense emotional response or triggered by your past.

Think for a moment about what might be the result of a sensitive person who does not have the tools to tend their emotional garden. We all need nutrients and nurturing to live a balanced and healthy life, and without effective self-care practices, we start to lose our life force energy. We may start to lose the essence of ourselves and grasp on to unhealthy coping mechanisms. We may click into survival mode because of the inevitable yet completely natural messes of modern-day life. This book is for anyone who has tried to let go of suffering and has not been able to do so yet.

In this book, I will teach you how to use EFT for yourself with my seven-step recipe to quiet the inner critic, understand how it works in the brain and in the body's energy system, and how you can make a massive upgrade in your life in the areas of health, love, and finances. EFT can even be helpful for tapping into your own divine creativity and increasing your productivity by completely getting out of your own way. I will sprinkle in EFT education throughout the book as I weave in inspiring and tender real-life stories of my own and those of my clients and friends. You will also find exercises you can use for self-discovery and protocols to follow no matter what topic you choose to tap on, including a road map at the end for making your wildest dreams come true. I will share with you the mystical and mysterious elements of tapping and I am also going to give you a step-by-step guide and exact recipe for the process.

As you learn about the wonderful world of tapping, I encourage you to use this book however you see fit. If you are in perfect health, rich beyond your wildest dreams, happily relishing in self-love, and surrounded by healthy relationships, you can take what you need and leave the rest. If you have picked up this book to learn more about tapping and helping others, I encourage you to explore the book in its entirety. Something may click into place, put the pieces together in a different way, or ideas may pop out to you that you can use for your clients, students, colleagues, friends, or family. If you are an EFT tapping skeptic, I welcome you. I encourage you to suspend your disbelief and entertain the magical, outside-of-the-box ideas, where anything is possible for you and the ones you love.

This book is organized into three parts:

Preparing the Soil: Learning about EFT, and the *how, what, when, where,* and *why* of EFT.

Seeding: Exploring specific areas of life where you can apply tapping to upgrade your reality. These sections will have journaling questions at the end for self-reflection.

The Harvest: Real action steps you can start using today to upgrade your experience.

If you would like to get started right away, you can find some free tap-a-long videos on my YouTube channel "Tapping with Steph," and examples of tapping scripts and resources on my blog (stephdodds.com). I would encourage you to tap along with YouTube videos just for experimental purposes, as tapping is best learned by doing, experimenting, practicing, and feeling the difference in your own body. This way, you can feel the difference in real time instead of imagining a possible outcome.

I would also recommend getting a fresh new notebook to be your EFT journal so you can use this material as a workbook to track your progress and for personal reflection.

I am so glad you picked this book up because you deserve to feel better and to feel freer. If you are ready to be in control of your emotions instead of them having control of you, I welcome you on this journey. You are worth this time. I won't try to love-bomb you here, but give it to you straight. If you are a *sensitive superhero*, you are powerful. And if you have haters or people who tease you for being sensitive, that has everything to do with them and not you. They may be jealous of your light. It is not easy being sensitive. It is pretty challenging. You deserve to experience this life with more snort-laughing joy, more presence, and more freedom in your day-to-day experience.

The motivation for this book comes from my heart. Think of this as a helpful step-by-step guide to tapping for sensitive people filled with real-life examples. Emotional Freedom Techniques is a tool that can help us grow and blossom into the beauties that we are. Welcome to the garden party!

1: Being Sensitive

"I've learned that people will forget what you said,
people will forget what you did, but people will
never forget how you made them feel."

—Maya Angelou

Thank goodness for the work of Elaine N. Aron, PhD, who is not only a highly sensitive person herself, but is a psychotherapist, a best-selling author, and is responsible for bringing awareness to the personality trait of being an HSP (highly sensitive person). In her book *The Highly Sensitive Person*, she mentions that culture plays a large role in how sensitivity is valued. Sensitive people tend to have low self-esteem, are viewed as abnormal, and grow up believing that something is innately wrong with them. They often feel misunderstood and misperceived. When I personally watched the documentary *Sensitive: The Untold Story* highlighting Elaine's work, I felt deeply seen and understood, and immediately texted my *sensitive superhero* buddies to *"go watch this documentary right away."*

Eline's work teaches us that being sensitive is not a disorder, but an innate temperament trait that is found in both men and women. She has also shown in her research that 20 percent of the population is *highly sensitive*, which wouldn't be the case unless it had some survival value. In certain situations, paying attention is valuable. She lets us know that sensitive people deeply process information, notice things more intensely and pick up on things that most people ignore or miss. Sensitive people are deep thinkers, intuitive, empathetic, creative, and natural leaders when they are nourished in the right environment, and they are a huge contribution to society. Elaine's research also shows that therapies like counseling are more effective for sensitive people, and when they have the right support around them, the sky's the limit for their growth and success.

Overstimulation and feeling overwhelmed are disadvantages of this trait. Sensitive people tend to have a harder time navigating the workplace, especially with unsupportive bosses. They also tend to struggle with self-love and self-acceptance and suffer from certain health issues due to burnout. This is where EFT tapping can come in and be helpful as our culture is not always prone to supporting our *sensitive superheroes* and giving them an environment to flourish in. Tapping can be a tool to help sensitive types let go of any distress they are feeling so they can get back to embodying their superpower again, sharing their gifts with the world from a calm and peaceful place.

Certain plants are more sensitive to their environment than others. Not all of us have thorns built in like roses, protective oil like poison ivy, or sharp needles like cacti. Some of us are just a little pickier and prefer not to be messed with. Plants can be particular about temperature, how much water they want, and have a preference about how much sunlight they would like to experience throughout the day. We do not suspect that there is anything wrong with the plant for being sensitive or gossip about how hydrangeas should not be so high maintenance. We gather all of the right materials to put that plant in an optimal environment to flourish and be happy. Just like plants, sensitive people can absolutely flourish in the right environment, with the right support around them.

You may identify as a highly sensitive person or simply feel sensitive at times. When observers see an HSP expressing emotion, they usually have one of three looks on their faces:

1. The "really? Tears now? Are you OK?"

2. The absolutely blank stare of indifference.

3. Tears welling up in their eyes because they are feeling the same energy of deep emotion. Every now and then, they see another sensitive soul looking back at them.

Sometimes sensitive types can feel guilty about not spending more time with the people they love. They are often zapped of energy and need more time to be alone for downtime to decompress. Balancing all of life's responsibilities is challenging and some sensitives often feel like their relationships don't get enough of them because they need to conserve energy.

If you look at sensitivity through an astrology lens, you may even consider being an air sign (Gemini, Libra, and Aquarius) or a water sign (Cancer, Scorpio, and Pisces) enough to be considered sensitive. In the school of human design, you might be someone who does not have their emotional center defined, and you can't separate yourself from what everyone else is feeling . . . all of the time. Some believe the idea that we are not born with a highly sensitive personality, but it is forged through a series of events and conditioning. These experiences were what we needed to become sensitive, as a brilliant self-defense mechanism. Therefore sensitivity comes as a result of traumatic experiences because you needed to be hypervigilant at some point, in order to protect yourself from anything bad ever happening again.

As I present the material in this book, I'm not here to diagnose you, or here to tell you who you are. You are the *YOU* expert. This is not a textbook either, but a teaching memoir of my own stories and those of my clients' perseverance, understanding, compassion, aha moments, and breakthroughs. I'm simply here to show you that there may be an easier way and that feeling emotionally free is absolutely possible for sensitive types and for all.

Just for good measure, let's review some definitions we will be talking about moving forward:

Crying

Crying is the act of tears and liquid coming out of the ducts beneath the eyeballs. Descriptive possibilities include weeper for a person who weeps, crier for a person who cries, and bawler for a person who bawls. Crying is a release of energy, and people often feel better after releasing a good cry. Tears can be produced by happiness, sadness, anger, watching a touching movie, and so on. A beautiful sunrise can elicit tears as well as deep grief about a loss. Crying, as you know, gets a bad rap. Even in situations when it is appropriate to cry, others will instruct, "Don't cry, don't cry." Social stigmas and labels can follow folks around, like "cry baby," even though crying is completely natural.

Sensitivity

What most people think of as being sensitive is = being overly emotional.

What sensitivity could actually mean is:

1. Being highly intuitive and empathetic
2. Being hyperaware
3. Being receptive
4. Being extremely observant
5. Caring deeply about others and the world
6. Having strong emotional reactions
7. Loving deeply
8. Feeling all of the feelings possible, most of the time

Sensitive Superheroes

Sensitive superheroes are people who have not seen their sensitivity as a gift in the past, but now recognize their sensitivity as a strength. They are people who set good boundaries, take good care of themselves, and are unapologetically themselves whether others understand them or not. Sensitive people have usually overcome trauma in their past, are highly intelligent, are heart-centered individuals, natural healers, and have a desire to help others.

Not Feeling Anything

I have only been bored two times in my whole life. I have always been incredibly easily entertained. It seems as though there is always something to ponder, to learn, to explore, to experience. The first time I remember experiencing boredom was when I was driving across the country on a road trip. At one point I had listened to three books on Audible, and could no longer tune in to the radio as I was driving through the center of Wyoming. As the road stretched on and on, I thought to myself, wow, I'm actually bored for the first time. I was grateful to notice the contrast between either being provoked by strong emotions or playing with a simple idea. By this time I was aware that even a little bit of stimulation is plenty.

The second time I experienced boredom, I was away for the weekend during a yoga teacher training graduation. This training was about six months long, and for our final weekend, we were whisked away to Lake Tahoe and our teacher informed us that we would be sitting in meditation pretty much all weekend. This would end up being about twenty hours of meditation total. Cool, I thought to myself, I've always wanted to dedicate this kind of time to meditation. I am not sure if you have ever meditated this long, but I was a beginner at the time. Beginner meaning the longest amount of time I dedicated to meditation was about ten minutes. As I sat on my cushion, on the hardwood floor, trying not to think about how sitting this way may be affecting my knees, I experienced every emotion. And I do mean everything . . . from total peace . . . to total annoyance, from anger to disgust, from feeling claustrophobic to impatient, from envy to what I think the monks mean by peacefully empty, with no thoughts at all. On the second day, about four hours into meditation, I came to a point of not being able to feel anything. This was not the peacefully-empty-monk feeling, but not being able to feel anything, like my feelers were somehow turned off. I thought to myself, wow, this is what it must be like to not feel everything and be constantly having *the feels*. At that moment I realized that even though I've always been sensitive, and I've always been a crier, I actually prefer a life where I can feel fully, all of life's experiences. Our feelings and emotions are our internal guidance system, and they are there for a good reason. It would be nice to feel all of life's emotions without being overwhelmed, however. I do not believe that the grass is greener on the other side; not feeling is not better, no matter how enticing it sounds. Being an emotionless robot does not sound like a good time either.

People who are not sensitive are missing out. A friend of mine, Jane, is not very sensitive. She is not able to read a room or experience self-awareness when she is rude to someone in her life. She has had a hard time in relationships and has a lack of empathy and understanding toward other people and where they might be coming from. She truly does not know how to put herself in other people's shoes to gain more perspective. Another friend of mine is very frustrated because he has a hard time connecting with others. He desperately wants to feel things but says he feels numb and has a hard time caring about anything besides himself. He shares this genuinely, as he would like to feel more, but doesn't believe he is wired that way. I tease him that his experience is a gift and that if most of my clients had one wish, it would be that they could not feel as much. But his one wish is to feel a deep connection with others, and even with himself.

Tears as Medicine

Your tears are powerful; they are medicine. Your tears can give you something that nothing else in the world can. Your tears have purpose and so do you. Tears are simply a release of energy and there is no greater medicine than tears. No pill can do what tears can do; no prescription can provide that kind of relief or healing. No amount of salve can soothe what needs to be released out of your mind, body, and spirit. Your tears are actually a gift, sacred water cleansing you and clearing you from the past. It is my honor to offer these teachings, so you can practice on your own, and get the full medicine of your tears. I am guessing that if you cry, you are not weak at all, but strong as hell. The sensitive people I know are usually extremely strong, highly intelligent, and are creative problem-solvers. On your own, or with a skilled practitioner, you can move through emotions, release them, and feel the appropriate amount of feelings for the moment. True emotional freedom comes from within, and this technique can help you get there on a daily basis. Feeling more grounded, more stable, and just more excited to be your beautifully sensitive, empathic, tender (*or whatever*) version of you is possible.

Lillian

I have a friend, Lilian, who is sensitive like me. One day we were both tearing up listening to a story a friend was sharing in our women's drum circle. The woman was sharing about one of her clients losing her daughter to cancer at the young age of sixteen. She was sharing all the medical procedures they tried, the alternative healing they tried, the anguish and family drama that surfaced during this difficult path. She shared that sometimes the highest healing is passing away. I looked over at my friend and we both had wells of liquid forming in our eyes. We looked at each other and without speaking, gave each other a look. Really? Tears again? Sheesh. Lillian then said to me, "I read in an article today that said that people who cry are actually incredibly emotionally intelligent. So I just view these tears as meaning we are really super smart." Then we both burst into laughter. Well, I guess we are freaking valedictorian geniuses.

The Ones Who Cry Just a Little Bit More

Even though I am a fairly spiritual person now, I grew up being a bit of a religious mutt. My dad came from a Mormon family. My mom, who was raised Lutheran, remarried a Jewish man when I was eight years old. When I would stay at a friend's house for a slumber party on a Saturday night, I would go to Catholic church Sunday morning with my friend's family. I feel lucky that religion was never imposed on me, or pushed in my face; it was more of an invitation to go shopping. Like going to a clothing boutique, I felt like I could try on that religion's coat for a bit and walk around the store to see if I liked it enough to take it home. I could even cut the sleeves off of the jacket and take whatever nuggets of wisdom I wanted with me, the wisdom that felt like a good fit.

I will never forget when my sixth-grade best friend, Beth, looked at me wide-eyed and said, "You've never been baptized? That's not good, Steph. I'm pretty sure you go to hell when you die if you haven't been baptized." I was eleven years old. This idea had never occurred to me, and I thought that maybe I should start looking into this baptism thing.

Then, I started going to church with my brother and his girl-friend. I think he was going to church with her to impress her and potentially get to third base, but he hesitantly let me tag along anyway. One day the pastor announced that there was going to be a baptism at the Peterson's house. Natalia Peterson was the one other girl from my class that I actually knew at this church. This was my chance not to go to hell, I thought. I contemplated my *why* long and hard, and this was some deep spiritual exploration for my eleven-year-old self, and I decided I was a *YES*. Fast forward two weeks, it was a lovely day by the Peterson's pool, where there were twenty kids, all under the age of sixteen, lined up to be baptized. They had music going, cupcakes, and even a guy making balloon animals. It was a party. They had each kid step up and read a few words before getting into the pool. Each one said a little something about loving Jesus, then were dipped in the pool by the pastor, and then everyone clapped as they came back up. When it was my turn, I remember being about to speak and being overcome with gratitude and love. A wave came over me. The thought of being reborn and starting new, acknowledging that I had faith in my heart in front of other people, felt like a big deal. It felt like I was surrendering to something bigger than myself for the first time. I was also realizing the magnitude of a sixth-grader deciding that this is what they wanted. Tears came as I squeaked into the microphone, "This feels really special. I want to be on Team God. Thanks for having me."

After I dried off and had a change of clothes, I went to give my dad a hug. He asked me, "How do you think it went?" I shrugged my shoulders and told him how embarrassed I was that I had cried, as I rolled my eyes. He patted me on the back and gave me a hug and said, "You know what, Steph, I've always liked the ones who cry just a little bit more than the rest."

As my dad would say, being sensitive is "not for sissies." It is definitely not easy to be so deeply affected and stimulated by everyday life experiences. You feel things, you know things (even if you are not sure how you know), and you can get easily wiped out by other people's stuff, big crowds, loud sounds, and even feel others' feelings.

If you feel overwhelmed by your sensitivity or have been judging yourself harshly for having this trait, you are not alone and it is time for a whole lot of self-compassion. Sociologist Judy Singer teaches us the term *neurodiversity*, which refers to the concept that there is no one "right" way of thinking, learning, and behaving. I hope in my sharing these stories from my own life and those of my clients and friends, you will be able to know without question that you are not alone. Being sensitive is the new strong, and now is the time for you to step fully into your strength.

2: An Introduction to Emotional Freedom Techniques

"Be who you are and say what you feel, because those who mind don't matter, and those who matter don't mind."

—Bernard M. Baruch

Every good gardener needs the right set of tools: a shovel, a watering hose, gardening gloves, and so on. The good news is, once you learn about the process of tapping and feel how effective it can be in your own experience, this technique will always be at your fingertips and available to you. Literally, all you need are your hands and fingertips, and a body to tap on.

The key to mastering this technique is practice, practice, practice. Whether you are new to tapping or have been tapping for years, this is very important groundwork for understanding what, when, how, where, and why anyone would want to incorporate this practice into their self-care routine. I would encourage you to approach this information with curiosity instead of feeling pressure to remember it all. In the words of my EFT teacher and mentor, Rob Nelson, "Imagine that you are soaking in the hot tub of knowledge and that you are absorbing the perfect amount of information that you need at this time."

Why Tapping

Let's start with why anyone would want to do this unfamiliar tapping business on your face and body. The answer to this question is simply to suffer less, feel better and enjoy the essence of life more. That may sound dramatic, but it's true. What would your life be like if you did not feel the emotional charge from your past experiences and traumas and were truly emotionally free? What would be possible for you if you didn't have any phobias or fears keeping you stuck? How would things look different if you fully loved yourself, liked yourself, and believed that you are worthy of amazing things happening to you? What if you deeply knew that your sensitivity was a gift instead of feeling embarrassed or shameful about it? OK, one more question: What if you were able to feel your feelings, and not let them take over your day, or week, or hold all of your attention? Your answers to those questions are examples of the *why* because this precious life is too short to be in your way any longer.

We are like fish swimming in water. The water is our beliefs and our emotional state, and we cannot see the water even though it is all around us all of the time—it is simply what is. If you asked the fish how the water is that it is swimming in, the fish might say, what water? Our life experience may be murky with intense emotions, negative thoughts, and limiting beliefs around any given topic. These ideas may not even be our own, but ones we have adopted or have been passed down to us. Tapping is simply a way to filter out the emotional junk that is keeping us stuck, and mucking up our peace. It creates space around the belief giving us a chance to see if we would like to keep that belief or throw it out. When we tap on what is wrong, or perceived to be wrong, or simply what is distracting us, we are able to come into the present moment and see with clarity. Tapping acts like a leaf catcher for a pool, scooping out the debris that is cluttering our water so we can see better, swim better, and have more access to joy and our own wisdom.

What Is EFT Tapping?

EFT stands for Emotional Freedom Techniques. Yes, there is an *s* on the end of techniques because there is a collection of useful techniques and tools available under the umbrella of EFT. EFT tapping is a self-soothing, stress-relief practice that is often referred to as an emotional form of acupuncture. It tends to work quickly and effectively to discharge emotional distress, interrupt negative thought patterns, and lower the charge of traumatic memories, which helps us be free of the lingering effects of our past. Weird and fabulous things can happen with this simple tool like headaches going away in as little as ten minutes with anger evaporating, and compassion easily replacing it.

Tapping can also create massive upgrades in our life and mind-set because it helps us release the effects of emotional distress and limiting beliefs that we may have created a long time ago. In the process of EFT, we speak out loud the negative reference points about anything that might be bothering us as we tap along the meridian points on the physical body in a sequence. Meridians are lines of energy running through the body, and we stimulate them all quickly by tapping on them with our fingertips. Essentially we focus on the "negative" when we tap, so we are able to acknowledge it, be with it, and release it if it is safe and appropriate to release. We want to name what is *"wrong"* or *"perceived wrong"* when we tap, so we are able to lower the emotional charge around it and let it go, as best as we can. The creator of tapping, Gary Craig, says that it often works when nothing else does.

A Brief History of EFT

It all started in the 1970s with a psychologist by the name of Dr. Roger Callahan. Purely out of personal interest, he found himself studying the traditional Chinese medicine practice of acupuncture. He made an accidental discovery one day while working with one of his patients, Mary, whom he had been working with on her water phobia for about eighteen months. In the EFT world, this urban legend is referred to as *The Mary Story*. Mary had a pretty severe water phobia for most of her life which, as you can imagine, caused many problems for her including drinking water and bathing. She had tried many therapies, and nothing seemed to help. In traditional psychotherapy, phobias are one of the more complicated conditions to cure.

One day at his home office in Santa Barbara, California, Mary mentioned that every time she even thought about water, she would get a terrible pain in her stomach. Dr. Callahan had just been learning about the stomach meridian in acupuncture, and so he said, "Why don't you just tap your stomach meridian point here under your eye?" She did this and boom! She ran outside to the swimming pool in his backyard, jumped in and started splashing around in the pool, saying, "It's gone, it's gone!" He thought she may have been losing her mind, but in fact it was a pivotal moment. Mary's phobia was gone.

After the success with Mary, Callahan knew he had discovered something extraordinary and began investigating tapping on different acupuncture points to treat different maladies and he called his new technique *Thought Field Therapy*. He was continuously getting unheard-of results with the specific algorithms for the tapping points to treat emotional issues and began teaching his technique.

About ten years later, in the late '80s, another wonderful physiotherapist, Dr. Francine Shapiro, was creating a similar mind-body technique called EMDR, Eye Movement Desensitization and Reprocessing. EMDR is a bilateral stimulation of the body, moving eyes back and forth, to break/release/relieve psychological trauma in a given way. She was getting notable results as well and knew that if she ever wanted to get her modality to hold credibility in the formal psychotherapy world, she would need to back it up with many studies. She did seven years of double-blind hard science studies proving the efficacy of EMDR. Once she had the body of research, then she presented it in 1995, it was accepted, and is now in practice around the world to this day. Unlike EFT, you need to be a licensed therapist to study and practice EMDR. The alternative healing world owes Dr. Shapiro a debt of gratitude for scientifically proving the mind-body connection and paving the way for the rest of us.

Meanwhile, Dr. Callahan did not conduct similar studies and was getting "booed" off the stage at psychology conventions, literally. People called him a "quack" and "fraud" and said there was no way you could possibly fix a phobia in minutes. Luckily he did not give up and continued to teach his methods. He actually charged $100,000 to learn Thought Field Therapy, and fortunately Gary Craig was one of the guys who wrote him a $100,000 check to learn this method.

Gary was an extremely bright, self-made millionaire, who was an NLP (Neuro-Linguistic Programming) Master and very interested in personal growth. He was retired and writing his own coaching programs when he found Dr. Callahan. He had gone to Stanford on a football scholarship and trained as an engineer, but never worked as an engineer. When he was learning Thought Field Therapy, he brought his engineering mind to the process and found ways to dramatically simplify it. In TFT, if someone has a particular problem, through a series of complicated algorithms, one would find out which tapping points to stimulate for their particular problem. For example, if someone was experiencing grief about their pet dying, they would get a printout of the algorithm recipe, which would tell them which point to tap on and in what order. And if someone had grief about the loss of a friend, it would give you a completely different algorithm recipe, and which tapping points to use. Even though they are similar situations, his technology would come with completely different instructions. There was also a twenty-minute process of muscle testing, to see if the individual was psychologically reversed, meaning did they really want to keep their program instead of letting it go.

Gary Craig was just being his brilliant self when he found a way to make TFT extremely accessible, and created an abbreviated form of it, which we call EFT today. I imagine Gary Craig scratching his head and thinking, huh? This means we will need to do everything by trial and error. Gosh, we are using the same tapping points; why don't we just tap all the points in a circle instead of tapping a few and seeing if it works? Instead of checking if someone is psychologically reversed via muscle testing for twenty minutes, why don't we assume that everyone is reversed? He came up with his own incredibly simplified protocol and shared it in an eighty-page manual that he put on the Internet for free. I believe it is still available on his website, emofree.com.

Today, millions of people are tapping all around the world. Teachers are leading tapping in their classrooms with their students, psychotherapists are helping their clients lower anxiety with tapping, and even the US Veterans Administration approved EFT as a recommended treatment for PTSD, pain, depression, and a handful of other related conditions.

Some people may think Nick Ortner created EFT because in 2008 he and his family launched the World Tapping Summit, and got the word out about tapping to the masses. Every year interviews are conducted with experts using EFT on various topics including self-compassion, chronic stress, and financial issues. The Tapping Solution app, which has been downloaded in 130 countries, has over five million tapping meditation recordings played.

The healing world owes Gary Craig a debt of gratitude for this amazing work. We also owe tremendous gratitude to all of those healing arts angels who are paving the way for us, doing clinical trials, and proving the effectiveness of this work and finding creative ways to share it. Who knows, maybe *YOU* will be part of the history in the making in the EFT world.

How Does EFT Work?

There are two ways to talk about how EFT actually works: the way it works in the brain, and how it works energetically in the body. Depending on your learning style and who you are talking to about it, you may prefer to use one of these approaches over the other.

Brain Stuff

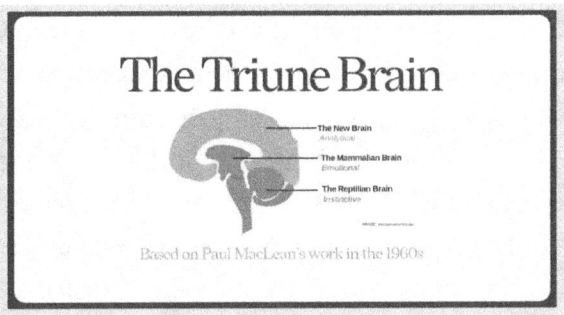

The human brain is extremely complex, but thanks to Paul McLean's work in the 1960s, we are going to think of the brain in three basic parts: the reptilian brain, the limbic brain, and the neocortex.

The reptilian brain controls our physiology, and it all happens so subconsciously we don't really need to think about it. For example, the reptilian brain is in charge of digesting our food, growing our eyebrows and fingernails, regulating our body temperature, and pumping our blood. When considering the reptilian brain, think about how alligators are not very concerned with their offspring. Mama alligators are pretty good parents, carrying up to fifteen baby eggs in their mouth to store in the protective cool mud, but the daddy alligators tend to eat the baby hatchlings. The reptilian brain has a very *eat or be eaten* vibe. The limbic brain, or mammalian brain, is our emotional and feeling brain. This part of the brain is very different, and is referred to as the dog brain. A pack of wolves, for example, has a much bigger investment in their young, socialization, and community. The limbic brain is where stress is handled. The neocortex is the rational, thinking brain. When you think of *neo*, think new: *new* ideas, learning, and so on.

The limbic brain is where stress is handled; this is where our fight, flight, and freeze response happens. The limbic brain is nonverbal, so it can't understand the content and context of the spoken word. For example, if you remember the way Charlie Brown's mom sounds, you can hear her talking but not be able to make out what she is saying. It just sounds like *whan whan whan . . ."* This is similar to how the limbic brain hears us and our self-talk. When someone is having an emotional upset, talking and talk therapy can be helpful, but sometimes it is not enough. Talk alone is often not enough to release the distress and trauma out of the physical body. This is why we talk *and* tap. Essentially EFT hacks into the emotional brain through the reptilian brain, sending a message that "all is well" and it is safe for us to relax. By tapping we break the connection to the perceived threat.

Tapping can disarm the fear response, so we can let go of trauma and not continue to replay, reenact, and recreate it day-to-day. Emotions are energy in motion, and all have their purpose. Emotions only become a problem when they get stuck, or when it doesn't feel safe to express them. As we tap, we verbally speak out loud the negative thoughts, feelings, and emotions related to the upset. We tap in order to communicate with the amygdala (the fear center of the brain) in order to send the message "I am safe, it is OK for me to relax" and clear our energy field.

Energy

It is important to talk about how we are all made up of energy—EFT tapping is considered Energy Psychology. Energy Psychology (EP) is a collection of mind-body approaches for understanding and improving human functioning. EP focuses on the relationship between thoughts, emotions, sensations, and behaviors, and known bioenergy systems (such as meridians). You can learn more about Energy Psychology at www.energypsych.org.

We always need to be clearing and cleaning our energy. Just like taking a shower, cleaning the house, or emptying the lint trap in the clothes dryer, keeping our energy-body clean and clear is vital to our health, well-being, progress, and overall feeling good. If we don't do this we can accumulate build-up, and we can get blocked. We can let our metaphorical garden weeds get out of control. If we don't keep our energy clear, we are likely to allow small bothersome incidents to continue to throw us off like thinking about that lady who was rude to us at the grocery store four days earlier. I would like you to start thinking of EFT tapping as if it is energy maintenance. Even if we have the cleanest, purest of energies, we still live in this world with lots of wild and unruly energies, judgments, and opinions swirling about: some positive and some negative. The good news is that there is nothing wrong with you if dust accumulates. It is empowering to realize that this process is natural; there is no defect. It really is a part of life and the work will never end.

When I talk about energy, this is not some woo-woo concept, but actual energetic frequencies measured with scientific equipment that provides actual data. Do you know that *beep beep* sound you hear when you hold a friend's hand in the hospital? No one finds that to be woo-woo, but that is measuring the energy frequency of the heart. If you are a sensitive person, you may be able to *FEEL* this energy, no matter how subtle. Have you ever walked into a room and it felt "off" or "icky"? No explanation; you can just sense it. Or have you seen someone smile while entering a room, and you can literally see the room light up?

In Western medicine, we go about helping someone feel better like we're building a fire. We schedule an appointment with a doctor, perhaps we try medicine or therapy, have follow-up appointments, and the doctor might say, "Call me in six weeks and let me know how you're feeling." You wait and see how that particular medication affects your body or have your broken arm wrapped up in a cast, and keep an eye on it. We gather the materials, light the matches, stoke the fire, and hopefully get it roaring and sustainable. With Energy Psychology, instead of building a fire, it's more like flicking on the light switch. The light bulb can turn on instantly when we're working in the energetic realm.

Tapping can help us get our energy flowing properly and take out the trash of the energetic junk and static we might be holding on to consciously or unconsciously. Any emotional upset can cause disruptions in our energy field. If we do not clear it and clean those disruptions, they can continue to repeat, attracting the same unpleasant experiences over and over again. I like to think about it like having batteries in a flashlight. The flashlight will not work if the batteries are installed in the wrong direction. EFT clears the disruption and gets our energy flowing properly again.

For example, picture a little horseshoe magnet. It's just a little piece of iron that's been magnetized. But there is a field around the magnet that is demonstrated when you hold up two magnets and try to put them together. You can sense the energy field as they push against each other. That is their energetic field. Our energy system is actually a field of energy. And there's not just one; there are many fields. Every organ in our body has its own energy field. The brain generates energy all the time, as we constantly think thoughts. The field extends past our bodies, and we have the technology to measure this now. You can learn more about this at www.heartmath.org. The heart field is the strongest, and it can extend measuring ten feet out from the body. So the disruptions in our energy system or energy field are reflected as unresolved traumas, unexpressed emotions, anything that causes suffering, and that's what we're tapping on. That's what is blocking our flow of energy. That disruption is actually the kink in our garden hose: frustration, anger, sadness, and so on.

If you ever watched little kids move through emotions, they'll be crying one second, happy the next. Children are quite fluid in their emotions compared to adults, as adults have years of learning how to stuff emotions down or "keep it together" so they can function at work, or if they are in a situation where it does not feel safe to express emotion.

For example, if I'm at a party, and somebody steps on my toes, it's appropriate for me to say, "Hey, get off my toes!" and feel anger. But if I grew up in a household where it doesn't feel safe to express anger or speak up for myself, I might just cower and back up, and try not to cause any trouble. This is the disruption that we are trying to clear, from those times when the emotions got stuck.

An example of how powerful a shift in our energy can be is the story of Brian. Brian called me for a quick tapping session before he had a court date. He had been in a nasty custody battle for the last two years with his ex-wife and he was filled to the brim with fear. On the FaceTime call, I could physically see the panic in his face. "What if I say something wrong?" he said. "What if I lose my daughter forever? My crazy ex-wife is going to shut me out of my daughter's life." It was pretty obvious that his fear was a level 10 on a scale of 1 to 10, so I told him to take a deep breath and tap along with me:

> [Setup statement] *"Even though I have this fear, I am afraid I'm going to lose my daughter forever; I'd love to get this fear out of my system as best as I can, at least for the next hour during court."*

> [Reminder phrases] *"This fear, all of this fear I have, I am totally freaking out, I am a mess, my relationship with my*

daughter is riding on how this goes. I choose to know this fear is trying to help me, and I have all of this fear because I love my daughter so much. I am acknowledging this fear right now and letting myself feel it, so I can be as calm and grounded as possible in court right now. This fear is not going to be helpful in there, so I would like to let go of whatever I can at this moment, so I can be peaceful and clear for the next hour."

After about ten minutes of tapping, Brian looked clear and confident. He said, "Well, I am just going to represent myself as best as I can, and the rest is out of my control; I am just going to have to trust the universe and know this is going to turn out OK." He said his fear was now at a 3 out of 10. (Not bad for just ten minutes.) His energy had shifted. By tapping on his fear, we were able to acknowledge it and dissolve most of it, so he was not bringing it to the situation with him.

Now that we have explored the *why, what, and how* of EFT, it is time to learn the tapping points, basic recipe, and principles of the process to make tapping work for you.

3: Principles of the Process

"Between stimulus and response, there is a space. In that space lies our freedom and power to choose our response. In our response lies our growth and freedom."

—Viktor E. Frankl

In this chapter, we will continue to learn the *when, where, and how* of EFT tapping. I will give you a tried-and-true recipe that I teach all of my EFT practitioner students.

When to Use EFT

You can use EFT tapping anytime, and as often as needed. Every time you tap, something shifts. This may be an itty-bitty shift or a gigantic shift. A little shift might feel like one of those moments when your head tilts to the side and you say to yourself, *"Huh . . . I do feel a bit different, lighter, calmer, more centered and that issue I was worried about feels a little more distant now."* You may have something to think about and journal about at a later time, but for now, you were able to take the edge off of whatever distress you were tapping on. A big shift may stop you in your tracks; you may see the veil lifting, notice colors brighter, and may feel the breeze on your cheeks. You may, depending on the topic, need to tap on something every day. Sometimes, however, and hopefully, you will have such a massive shift that an entire issue becomes a complete nonissue.

For example, during one of my EFT trainings, a student of mine was ready to tackle a relatively big issue in a practice round. Jamie shared that she was struggling with a tremendous amount of guilt and worry because her daughter was in rehab and had struggled with drug abuse for years. She felt a 10 level of guilt on a scale of 1 to 10, as she put the blame on herself that her daughter was so messed up. We tapped and tapped on guilt; it went down a little bit, but no real breakthroughs. Then in one tapping round, we tapped, *"If only the tremendous amount of guilt and worry were actually helping my daughter, then I would worry ten times more! But this guilt and worry are not helping; in fact, it is probably making things worse. If this guilt and worry were helping, she would be cured by now. Maybe the best thing I can do for her is to visualize her healing and send her extra love."* Jamie looked like she had just seen where the leprechaun had been hiding the gold all of this time; you could see the "ka-ching" realization happen in real time.

"The guilt is gone," she said. "I love my daughter and would do anything for her. If that means not worrying, I am willing to do that. I am done with the guilt and the worry." The class was full of observers who blinked in amazement.

It is appropriate to tap in the morning to start your day off on the right foot, or at night in order to fall asleep or sleep better. If you are going through a stressful time or working on some big goals, tapping with a professional EFT practitioner once a week can be life-changing. You can also follow along with videos on YouTube any time throughout the day. You can tap anytime you get triggered about a particular event, or person, or have a disproportionate emotional reaction to anything. You cannot tap too much. So the answer to *when* to tap, is anytime! However much or as little you want to or are able to.

Here are the Tapping Points for a Tapping Sequence:

Where to Tap

1. Karate chop point (for setup statement)

2. Top of the head

3. Top of the eyebrow

4. Side of the eye

5. Under the eye

6. Under the nose

7. On the chin

8. On the chest/collarbone

9. On the ribs, below the nipple

10. Under the arm on ribs where bra line would be

11. On the front of the wrist

12. On the back of the wrist

13. Then back to the top of the head for the next round

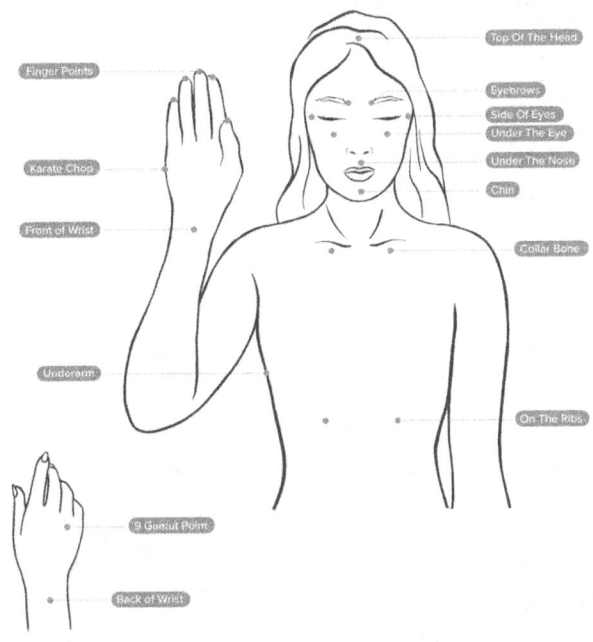

We are tapping on traditional Chinese acupuncture points. Each point has an organ/meridian line associated with it. I have many acupuncturists in my EFT trainings and they always contribute so much to the process with their knowledge.

One workshop attendee had been practicing acupuncture for thirty years. He shared with the group of acupuncture newbies that the reason you put the needle into certain places in the body is to open up that channel, that line of life force energy, so more positivity can flow through it. He compared it to a highway that was clogged up with traffic and blocked with construction. Stimulating that channel with a needle prick opens up the lanes, clears the construction (or obstruction) and the cars can drive easily again. The good news is you don't have to be an acupuncturist or even have knowledge of the meridian system in order for EFT tapping to work for you. But feel free to study all you like! We are simply stimulating these points with our fingertips.

How to Tap

Here is the basic EFT recipe:

<u>*Step 1:*</u> State the problem and find the main emotion surrounding it.

EFT may not be super helpful if you're having the best day of your life and you have no problems. Step one is to state your problem, know what you would like to work on, and discover "the problem" at the moment. For example, Sue is driving her car to work and she hits a traffic jam. Her boss just lectured her yesterday about being on time and she is presenting for a very important meeting today. She sees the traffic and automatically says, "Nooooooo!" to herself out loud in the car and the stress turns on. This is a good time to tap, as even if she gets there on time, chances are she will be a bit flustered for her meeting. Side note: I wouldn't recommend tapping while driving, but if you are stuck in traffic and not moving, go for it! Sue's problem = stuck in traffic. If Sue wants to help herself calm down with tapping, she will now need to see how she feels about this problem and measure its intensity. What emotion has come up? There may be many emotions here, but we want to see if we can find the main theme. She has determined that she is frustrated as she hates being late and she gave herself plenty of time to get to work. For any issue you are working on, a good question to ask is, "How do I know this is a problem?"

Step 2: Measure the SUD level of emotion.

Rate your emotional response to a particular topic on a 0 to 10 scale, with a 0 meaning this issue doesn't bother you at all, and 10 being big-time emotional distress or discomfort. We refer to this as a "SUD" level or "Subjective Units of Discomfort or Subjective Units of Distress." Sue will measure the "SUD" level, "How frustrated am I?" She determines she is an 8, pretty dang frustrated. The SUD level is simply a self-assessment, not a judgment. It is a way for us to measure where we start and how we progress through the tapping sequences. For some, this number will pop into your mind immediately, do not second-guess it; just go with the first number that pops up. For some, trying to rate how much emotion you have will be difficult. Do not overthink this step; this is simply a measurement to see if that tapping is helping or not. Do the best you can to give the emotion a number.

Step 3: Setup statement

The setup statement is an important step and the only place where you need to add a positive phrase. The blueprint for a classic setup statement is "Even though I ___(have this problem: fill in the blank) _____, I still deeply love and completely accept myself." For example, Sue's setup statement could sound something like this: "Even though I have this frustration, I can't believe I am stuck in traffic before my meeting today, I still deeply love and completely accept myself." If you have a hard time saying I deeply love and accept myself, I would encourage you just to try and say it even if you don't believe it yet. Here are also some alternative variations of setup statements if these options feel better for you.

More setup statement options:

- Even though I have this issue, I choose to forgive myself (*as best I can*).

- Even though I have this issue, I would like to get to a calm and peaceful place.

- Even though I have this issue, I would still like to feel good about myself and good about my life.

Step 4: Tap through the meridian points, speaking out the reminder phrases. Reminder phrases are simply speaking out the emotion and the different aspects of what you are going through. For example, Sue could say the following as she tapped on each point:

"All of this frustration."

"I have so much frustration right now."

"I can't believe I am stuck in traffic again."

"I tried everything I could to be on time today."

"That is why this is so incredibly frustrating."

"This is completely out of my control right now."

"This remaining frustration."

Complete a few rounds (a round is a whole round of tapping through points in a circle) of the negative statements, then finish up with the positive statements if you like. This works with emotions as well as limiting beliefs, which we will talk more about in chapter 13 when I introduce affirmation-based tapping. If at all possible, you want to end on a positive note.

Example of ending on a positive note of statement:

"Even though this sucks, and it is frustrating, I am still an awesome human being, even if I am late today."

"Even though I have this remaining frustration, what really matters is getting to my destination safely, and I will definitely be able to do that."

"Even though I don't have my whole life figured out right now, I love myself for being a caring person and caring if I do a good job at work. I can feel good about this; this is a positive thing."

Step 5: Remeasure your "SUD" level. It should go down a bit; it is even possible to get to 0! If the number is not going down, get more specific. A good question to ask is, "What makes this issue still a level 6 frustration?" Then pause and feel and listen. Therein lies the next part of our tapping script. This technique works better the more specific you are! Keep repeating steps 1–5 until you feel a shift, feel better, or sometimes can't even remember why you were upset in the first place.

Why Tap

We are like the Koi in the pond. The water is our beliefs and our emotional state, and we cannot see the water even though it is all around us; it is simply what *is*. Clearing our intense emotions, negative thoughts, and limiting beliefs around truly any topic, can leave us calm, centered, and clear-headed. Once our energy field is clear of the emotional disruption, we get to swim in wonderful water that's crystal clear. For example, if Sue does a few rounds of tapping to calm down, she may be able to see her next turn better, she can keep her confidence for her presentation, and most importantly, her self-worth is not tied up in a little mistake. And on an energetic level, maybe the cars will clear out of the way? Weirder things have happened with EFT; it is certainly worth a shot.

Focusing on the Negative

This is usually the hardest part for beginner tappers, the idea of focusing on the negative. Especially if you are a law of attraction type and a positive person by nature and do not want to utter one negative thing out of your mouth because then it might come true. I get it, you don't want to *put it out there* because we are truly powerful beings, and our thoughts, words, actions, and attitudes really shape our reality. I will always encourage others (and myself) to be positive, listen to motivational speakers, and keep the vibe high in your home space, in your thoughts, and in your words. But in the EFT world, we focus on the negative, and this is so we are able to release it as best as we can so that we can get back to the goodness. If you find it difficult to focus on the negative, perhaps you can shift the perspective here to focusing on what's strong, not what's wrong.

Let's say you and I met up for a fun Saturday of playing tennis. We have on our neon outfits, including sweat headbands, and are out there hitting the ball back and forth having a grand old time. Then I hit a great shot over the net; you run for it and trip and fall. You skin up your knee, and it looks pretty gross, and of course, it hurts. There is gravel, dirt, blood, and maybe even a very small leaf and twig sticking to your otherwise beautiful knee. Ouch. Luckily our nurse friend is there with her first-aid kit and is ready to help patch you up. What if our nurse friend sat you down to patch up your knee and just wrapped it up with gauze, without cleaning it, and just said, "Think positive and only focus on the good, and you will be fine, champ." This may be a little weird, and you might ask her, "Wait, won't this get infected?"

We focus on the negative with EFT so we are able to see it and clean out the gravel, dirt, blood, and possibly small leaf and twig, so that the wound may heal properly without anything stuck, without any scarring or infections. Does this hurt? Yep. It does kind of suck to focus on this "negative" in the short term; it hurts, it stings, it is uncomfortable, and it is really helpful to do in order to heal properly long term.

Focusing on the negative is really important when maintaining your emotional freedom garden. It would be really nice if we could just think positive and focus on the pretty flowers and what is going right, but, in the words of my grouchy garden plot neighbor, "Those weeds are not going to pull themselves." The good news is when we do the work and take the time to pull out the weeds when they pop up, the flowers flourish easier. The garden does not need to fight against itself, and the plants do not need to fight for space. When we pull out the "negative" weeds, it creates space for *MORE* positivity to be natural and effortless.

Reframing

Reframing is an opportunity to offer a new level of understanding and higher perspective on any given issue and is extremely helpful in the EFT world. When we are able to look at something with a new view or frame, it usually comes with a lot more compassion and self-love for the tapper. It can be difficult to do on your own, but with the right practitioner, it can totally flip whatever problem you are focusing on into a positive aspect. The intention of reframing is to experience a cognitive shift.

I was working with Amy one day, on a painful memory she had of seeing another mom yell at her own child out in front of the grocery store. It was years later at this point, but the image of the kid's dirty face and high-pitched cry were etched into Amy's mind. She did not know what to do at that moment and she expressed how painful it was to see the child and hear what the parent was saying to him.

She thought about the little one off and on, wishing there was something she could do to make his life better. We tapped and tapped on this memory. First, we tapped down the emotions with the memory (sadness and fear), and then we tapped on the visual details that she saw. Once those other aspects have less of a charge, this is the time when a potential reframe is the most effective.

We tapped, "*Even though I wish I could have helped that kid, and I fiercely wanted to protect him, I love that I have that deep intuitive instinct to protect children. I choose to know it is a good thing, not a bad thing, that I was upset by this scene. It would be really messed up if I just walked by and didn't care. Even though sometimes it totally sucks being a deeply caring person, I would rather be a deeply caring person than not be. I choose to take the wisdom from this incident and use it to be an even better mom to my son. I choose to use my intuitive instincts for good.*" Amy's eyes opened up and you could see the shift that happened. She was able to let go of the distress from the memory and instead of feeling helpless, felt grateful that she does have the maternal instincts that she possesses.

EFT & Trauma

The word *trauma* is becoming more and more mainstream as we have drudged through the 2020s and have found ourselves with a much bigger focus on mental health than ever before.

We are learning more and more about how we hold trauma in the body and how certain traits like codependency and people-pleasing may be a trauma response. Yet, if you ask ten people what the definition of trauma is, they may all give you very different answers. The definition from the American Psychological Association is as follows:

"*Trauma is an emotional response to a terrible event like an accident, rape, or natural disaster. Immediately after the event, shock and denial are typical. Longer-term reactions include unpredictable emotions, flashbacks, strained relationships, and even physical symptoms like headaches or nausea.*"

In the EFT world, we define trauma as anytime someone goes into a "freeze" response, as mentioned in chapter two. When humans have a stress response, three things might happen: we go into fight, where we are prepared to deal with the threat; we go into flight, where we flee or run from the threat; or we go into a freeze response. Freezing usually happens when fight or flight does not work. The freeze response is completely involuntary. We don't think, hey, how about I become frozen with shock at this moment? It just happens. Like a possum, we are prone to freeze and keel over and play dead, hoping that the threat will go away. Humans can go into a freeze response when we experience a real or perceived threat or even just a threat to our identity. In these modern times, one can go into a freeze response when receiving an email, a text, watching the news, or getting an unexpected bill in the mail.

A brilliant American therapist named Peter Levine had a great question: Why don't animals in nature get stress-related diseases? In his book *Waking the Tiger*, he discovered that animals *shake* in order to discharge the freeze response out of their system, getting out all of the adrenaline that gets stuck in the body. Animals usually do not die from stress, even when they are in constant threat of being their predator's next lunch. Animals shake and shake to get the stress out of their system and go back to doing their thing. For humans, on the other hand, it is not a part of our culture to do this. If there is some kind of natural disaster, someone usually comes by with a blanket and says, "Don't shake; it will all be OK." Essentially with the act of focusing on the *distress* and tapping on the body, we are stimulating this *shake it off* method.

Now that you have the basic recipe of tapping and know the principles of the process, you can use it at any time. You can carry this tool in the car with you or use it at the grocery store; you have all the tools at your disposal to be like Taylor Swift and *shake it off* yourself any time you need to.

4: Emotional Wellbeing & Maintenance

"But when we really delve into the reasons for why we can't let something go, there are only two: an attachment to the past or a fear of the future."

—Marie Kondo

Early on in my gardening days, I wanted to know every little thing there was to know about growing the perfect flowers, peppers, and especially pumpkins. I had a twinkle in my eye as I would try and drum up conversations with strangers at the local Tahoe nursery.

"How are your greens looking this year? What's your secret?" My boyfriend at the time was a very knowledgeable gardener and gave me my first pair of Felco pruners that year.

"First lesson," he said, "how to trim the energy suckers."

I looked horrified as he started to cut away at the yellow cherry tomato plant I was so proud of for being big and bushy. I stood there with my jaw dropped as I watched bountiful green branches being cut away. He said, "Do not worry, Steph, this is what is best for the plant." I wanted to believe him, but it was hard to imagine that this seemingly dramatic trimming was beneficial. After I gathered myself, he explained to me that the plant only has so much energy to expel, as all of us do. The plant can use its power to reach the tips and give life to the budding fruit, giving it nutrients and sustaining life. The plant puts its precious energy into keeping its budding bits and dying bits alive, giving itself a reasonable chance at survival. This is a short-term strategy and can deplete the plant in a way that leaves it average in size and production, spending its energy trying to keep what it has. If we trim those budding and dying bits away, it is not a loss for the plant, but the plant has the opportunity to keep its life force from its home base, from its source. This long-term strategy can be tough at first; it is painful to trim away the bits that may be siphoning energy. But when you do, the plant is free to grow bigger, stronger, and produce even more buds and fruit in the future.

Our energy is precious, just like a budding cherry tomato plant's is. Emotions can suck up a lot of our energy, especially if they are intense, sporadic, wild, or unruly. Each emotion that we feel is also natural, organic, valid, and has a purpose. Have you ever been really angry at someone? It's exhausting. It takes a ton of energy to be angry. Have you ever been so overwhelmed that it took the fun out of a positive activity? Tapping can help us trim the energy suckers out of our system, meaning any excessive emotions that are not helping any given situation that you might be in, and draining you instead of helping you be productive. You can use tapping to embody your life force energy in a powerful way that will make you stronger, just like that plant.

In this chapter, we will talk about some of the main emotions, and how they actually have a darn good reason for being there. I will share some tapping script examples with you as well, to help us reframe our experience, so we are able to move through each emotion properly. Why? Because tapping is a way for us to trim energy suckers from the subconscious. We may be expelling much more energy than we need to. For example, if I'm feeling like Sue, who is at a 10 out of 10 level of frustration about being stuck in traffic, I can tap, tap, tap for about ten minutes and feel so much better. Where did that extra frustration go? The energy it takes to feel a 10 out of 10 frustration comes back to the source, back to our center; I get to have my energy for me again. This factor alone is invaluable for sensitive people as we need our energy for our health, life force, and creativity. Without even knowing it, we could be expelling energy from a conversation we had yesterday, from being in a large crowd, or even watching the news. Even though it might be painful to focus on what is "wrong" initially, when we begin to tap, this is a way to cut away our energy suckers. It is possible to get your energy back from things, events, and people that have sucked it away in the past. Your life force comes from your roots, your center, which you need so that you can grow bigger, stronger, and produce more fruit in your own time. If we try to push these emotions down or ignore them, they do not go away. If we try not to feel what we really feel, we are fighting against a force of nature; under the surface, that is when our emotions can get stuck and create disruptions in our energy field and be draining us.

Emotions

Emotions are defined in the dictionary as "A natural instinctive state of mind deriving from one's circumstances, mood, or relationships with others. Also as a conscious mental reaction (such as anger or fear) subjectively experienced as a strong feeling, a state of a feeling, or an affective aspect of consciousness."

Although there are many, some of the main emotions are joy, sadness, anger, frustration, disgust, anxiety, excitement, overwhelm, and fear. They are normal and natural and only become a problem when they get stuck and cause a disruption in our body or energy field.

Growing up, I remember learning how to identify emotions. For example, seeing a worksheet with a variety of otherwise smiley faces making other faces with different emotions written under them: sad, angry, overwhelmed, frustrated, calm, neutral, and so on. I do not remember, however, learning to dive a bit deeper when it comes to these emotions. For example, why do we have them? Or once we do, what do we do with them and how do we move through them in a constructive way? I had always considered myself emotionally intelligent growing up, because I was deeply empathic and could feel others' feelings, but did not have many practical tools to help navigate through all of those feelings and tell if they belonged to me or others.

Perhaps somewhere inside of you, it does not feel safe to feel your feelings. Somewhere along the way, you learned you "shouldn't" be sad, angry, overwhelmed, and so on. I imagine it's kind of like these feelings get stuck somewhere in your being. Just like when a garden hose has a kink in it, emotions can get stuck, backed up, and block the flow.

Let's identify different types of emotions and how a sensitive person might experience them. Everything listed below is natural and on the typical spectrum of human emotional states that all healthy humans experience. Here are our garden-variety favorites: sadness, anger, fear, anxiety, frustration, overwhelm, grief, guilt, and shame.

Sadness

Feeling sad can be an overall heavy feeling like you are wearing a big wet blanket or walking through river mud in oversized boots. Sadness can also be very situational and be felt due to specific namable events of a loss, relationship heartbreak, disappointments at work, or even failing at a simple task. According to the National Institute of Mental Health, more than 17.3 million people in the United States suffer from depression as of 2017. Some believe this number has skyrocketed since the COVID-19 pandemic. Depression gets mistaken for sadness at times, and vice versa. Sadness can be felt in shorter time increments; depression can last months or even years. Sometimes people with depression do not know why they are depressed. Their symptoms are mistaken for fatigue, loss of interest, misery, and physical body aches. Sadness is a natural reaction and is appropriate to feel at certain times.

When my dear friend Sam lost her dog of twelve years, she was truly devastated. She was having trouble focusing at work and getting out of bed in the morning. She looked annoyed when I asked how sad she might be on a scale of 0 to 10. "Ten, duh," she murmured. We tapped and tapped together on the sadness and grief she was experiencing. After about twenty minutes, she was down to a 4 sad.

"I guess there is no hope for me then, still a 4," she reported.

I reminded her that our feelings have a damn good reason for being there. Feeling sadness about losing her sweet puppy is absolutely appropriate, so having a level 4 sadness seemed perfect. Our only goal was to tap away any excessive sadness that she did not need, the sadness that wasn't helping the situation. That is the sadness that was keeping her distracted at work, interfering with her everyday functioning, and the rest she needed to help her move through that time.

Reframing ideas for sadness: _"Even though I am feeling this sadness, I am glad I have the ability to feel so deeply. I am willing to feel this sadness, and let it move through me. It is completely understandable that I have this sadness at this moment. I honor my sadness, and I would like to come to a calm and peaceful place about this situation and in general."_

Anger

Anger can be ignited when something sacred has been violated. We are most often mad at ourselves for allowing the violation or angry with the perpetrator who caused the harm. Anger takes an extraordinary amount of energy to feel and hold on to and can escalate to rage. This can be a tricky emotion to navigate if we grew up in a home where we were not allowed to express anger, or someone else in the home was "the angry one." If anger is an unfamiliar feeling, it can be very uncomfortable.

One thing to remember is that anger is appropriate and has a purpose. If someone steals your bicycle while it is locked up in front of the grocery store, anger is an appropriate reaction. Believe it or not, tapping on anger can even be fun because it is such a release. Tapping is a place where you can say all the things that you really feel, even saying them with anger. Actually, I often encourage my clients to *tap and rant*. There is no need to be polite, politically correct, fair, or even make sense; it is just permission to get it all out of your system.

Reframing ideas for anger: *"Even though I am still feeling so much rage and anger, holding on to this is costing me dearly. Even though something sacred has been violated, and I have all of this anger about it, I have every right to have this anger, and I have every right to let it go. I would like to come to a place of forgiveness, even if they don't deserve it. I would like to get this anger out of my system, as best as I can."*

Fear

Oh fear, this powerful and primitive human emotion. Fear is both a universal biochemical response and a highly individual emotional response. Biochemical responses could be an increased heart rate, sweating, racing thoughts, and spikes of adrenaline. Fear can be highly individual also. For instance, one person may love dogs and another may have an extreme fear of them, most likely tied to previous experiences.

Fear really tries to be helpful as well, even though most of the time it is not. Fear this . . . fear that . . . stay safe! Look out! Fear surfaces where there is a real or perceived threat to our safety, the safety of others and even a threat to our identity or resources. Fear kicks us into a stress response: fight, flight, or freeze. Fear is always trying to do its job of keeping us out of harm's way. Tapping on fear is very helpful in turning down the volume knob on our stress response. We are able to feel the fear, acknowledge the fear, and then proceed.

Reframing ideas for fear: "*Even though I am feeling this fear right now, feeling fear is understandable at this moment. Even though this feeling of fear is pretty intense, I would just like to validate and acknowledge these feelings. I forgive myself for feeling this fear, and I love myself for wanting to feel safe. Even though having some fear is appropriate in this situation, I am willing to let go of any excessive fear that is making things worse.*"

Anxiety

Anxiety can be the other side of the coin of fear. Anxiety sufferers are usually familiar with thoughts of excessive worry, uneasiness, nervousness, and panic. Anxiety can be situational or it can also feel like an uneasiness that is always under the surface, not allowing a person to truly relax. For example, if someone has a big exam coming up or an event where you need to give a speech, anxiety can pop up like a game of whack-a-mole. Sometimes anxiety can come on suddenly, and escalate within minutes. When this happens, we call it a panic attack. If you have struggled with anxiety, you know it's the worst. Tapping has the potential to lower your feelings of anxiousness within minutes.

Reframing ideas for anxiety: "*Even though I am feeling this anxiety, I love this part of me that is trying so hard to keep me safe. Even though I am feeling all of this anxiety, and would love to just breathe in this moment, look around the room, and realize that there is nothing wrong in this moment. Even though this anxious feeling really sucks, I love myself for wanting to feel better.*"

Frustration

We all know the feeling of frustration; it usually comes when we are annoyed or upset, especially if we are not able to change or achieve something. It is difficult to see situations clearly, even right in front of our eyes, when we are filled with frustration. Oftentimes, sensitive people get frustrated with themselves because something affected them so deeply and they wish they didn't care. Frustration is also natural if we have tried to solve a problem ten times now, and we still can't seem to figure it out. Alternatively, tapping on frustration can lead to clarity, insight, and regaining your power and energy. It is very effective when you are really brutally honest with what you are frustrated about, and not trying to play it cool like something does not really bother you.

Reframing ideas for frustration: *"Even though I have this frustration, this frustration makes so much sense, and it is completely understandable that I feel this way. Even though I am feeling all of this frustration because I haven't met a suitable romantic partner yet, this frustration probably isn't helping me. If only this frustration were making my love appear faster, but it is probably what is keeping love at a distance, so I am willing to soften in my experience."*

Overwhelm

Overwhelm is probably the most useful thing for sensitive people to tap on because we can easily become overwhelmed by life. If we notice things more intensely, deeply process information, and feel overstimulated, overwhelm makes perfect sense and can often become our default setting whether we like it or not. Tapping on the aspects of what is currently overwhelming a *sensitive superhero* can help them to feel grounded, come back into the present moment, address one thing at a time, and proceed calmly, confidently, and gracefully.

Reframing ideas for overwhelm: "*Even though I am feeling over-whelmed, this truly is a lot of information to process, and feeling overwhelmed is completely understandable. All of these feelings I am experiencing right now are not my feelings; there is nothing happening at the moment to warrant them, so I am allowing myself to come back into this present moment and feel grounded. Even though it feels like there is too much on my plate at this moment, I am willing to take a deep breath in and out and put one foot in front of the other. I am a smart and capable human being and I can do anything I set my mind to.*"

Grief

Tapping on grief can help if you are going through a heart-break or a loss, although it is a little more tricky than the other emotions. Usually, when we tap we are trying to let go of any emotions that are causing problems, and we hope to let go of the excessive emotion. But grief is supposed to be there; there is no way around it, and we must go through it. Grief can also sneak up on you. You can be having a great day and then like a wave, something can pop up and remind you of a great loss, and you are back in grief again. Grief cannot be rushed. Grief requires patience and self-kindness.

Usually, I see one of two outcomes when tapping on grief: someone can feel much better and be smiling, or lots of tears start to flow and the grief comes in full force. Both of these options are healthy as you are moving through the emotion instead of avoiding it.

One of my clients, Bill, had stuffed down the grief of losing his mother twenty-five years earlier. His chronic fatigue finally nudged him to look at his grief and work on it. Like many who stumble upon tapping, he was willing to try anything. He reported that actually taking some time to be with his grief and look at it felt like finally vacuuming a house that had not been touched in twenty-five years. He told me once, "If there was anyone out there who would listen to my advice, I would tell them to deal with the grief they experience at the moment they feel it because, believe it or not, it is much harder to dig it up later, and to do a deep cleaning of it twenty-five years later." It took us a couple of months of weekly sessions, but soon Bill started to gain his energy back and started remembering his dear mother's life with pleasure instead of the pain of her death.

Reframing ideas for grief: "Even though I am feeling all of this grief, it is probably because I love so deeply. This person meant so much to me; it would be really weird if I did not feel this grief about this great loss. Even though I am not there yet, I am willing to take my time processing this grief when I am good and ready. Even though I am feeling this grief, I would like to remember this person with pleasure, instead of all this pain. They would have never wanted me to be so miserable."

Guilt & Shame

In Brené Brown's TED talk "Listening to Shame," she shares a simple yet profound way to help differentiate the experience of guilt and shame. Guilt means "I did something bad or I made a mistake" versus the heavyweight slugger of shame that is "I _am_ bad or I _am_ a mistake." Guilt is felt when someone has a sense of regret for something they have done, should have handled better, or something they believe is their fault. Shame is that inner critic, which can feel like a weighted blanket, usually letting you know that you are either not good enough, or says, _"Who do you think you are?"_

According to Brené's research, she has found that we all feel shame at some time or another. For women especially, we need to "do it all, and do it perfectly, and never let them see you sweat." When shame comes up, it is usually because of some unattainable, unrealistic or conflicting expectations of who we are supposed to be.

Sensitive people need to take good care of themselves when shame pops up, as we most likely have years of practice of feeling misunderstood, misperceived, and feeling out of place and then something happens to reignite those feelings. The only conclusion you might come to is "there is obviously something inherently wrong with me."

These feelings of guilt and shame can really harm your self-esteem, so some "self-loathing" tapping is extremely beneficial. When you are really struggling with guilt, shame, self-hatred, or not-good-enoughness, it's helpful to make a list of all the bad things you say to yourself. I know this sounds incredibly brutal, but remember we want to disrupt these thought patterns, say them out loud, and tap on them so they lose their power over you. In fact, when I am tapping with someone on their long list of critical self-talk topics, they usually end up laughing or admitting that the things they say to themselves sound ridiculous when spoken out loud. Often I get to see my client's eyes light up when they see that the inner critic is actually completely wrong about them, and the mean things it said are not even remotely true.

One day I was tapping with Kara on her inner critic of shame, and her list went something like this:

- Not good enough as a mom or a business owner.

- I should be better, smarter, and handle all of life's curveballs smoother.

- There must be something wrong with me.

- I don't have a difficult life; I am not sure why I am not happier.

- I don't deserve a good life. I will deserve it, once I am perfect.

- I am damaged goods (from a past memory).

- Who do I think I am to help other people?

- If people knew who I really am they wouldn't love me, and so on.

We tapped and tapped together. I knew she had a strong inner critic because we'd had a few sessions together already, but this time she burst out laughing. She looked at me and said, "You know what? My inner critic is so full of s***! It would be out of a job if I never listened to it. It is a professional bulls***ter!"

We want to validate all of our feelings with EFT, because feelings are, well, they are valid. But shame is a little different; this is the only feeling that we probably won't validate because you are actually wonderful. That is the actual truth of your being. As Jenn Sincero suggests in her book *You Are a Bad Ass,* "You are actually moonbeams and stardust in drag."

Reframing ideas for guilt & shame: "*Even though I am feeling this guilt, I would like to forgive myself as best as I can. Even though I feel like I should be doing a better job in life, and I 'should' myself all of the time, I would like to come to a place of self-acceptance today. Even though I am feeling this shame, this shame actually doesn't belong to me. I may have picked it up somewhere along the way. That other person, they are the ones who should feel bad for doing what they did, but I am stuck here feeling all of this shame for them. Even though I have this icky, shamey feeling, I don't really need to carry this shame anymore and I chose to feel better about myself and feel better about my life.*"

Here are some more reframe ideas that are "almost" emotions we can tap on as well:

Resistance

"Even though I am feeling so much resistance, I am just going to let myself feel this resistance and not fight it anymore. I fully accept my resistance, and I love myself for having it."

Judgment

"Even though I have been judging myself so harshly, and been so hard on myself, I still love and accept myself right now, as best as I can."

Annoyance

"Even though I am incredibly annoyed and agitated right now, I love myself for wanting peace and quiet. I am honoring how I feel in this moment, as it is completely understandable."

I would like you to think about this information when you are doing the maintenance work of pruning, cutting away, shortening, snipping, and trimming of your emotional freedom garden. Yes, it might hurt at first. Some part of you, deep in your subconscious mind, might want to hold on to that suffering because it is all you have known. I am not saying that we are just throwing stuff out to get rid of it, or even that you can get rid of your stuff. But you can take the pain out of it, so your trauma feels like distant memories instead of in your face. If you have the courage to feel your emotions, tap on them, and cut away those energy suckers now, your life will feel richer and more fruitful. Identify it, tap on it, and cut away those energy suckers now. It will increase your fruitfulness, growth, and all-around well-being in the long term.

SEEDING

5: Health & the Physical Body

"A memory without the emotional charge is called wisdom."

—Dr. Joe Dispenza

From headaches to hair loss, in my private practice, I find that tapping works about half of the time when it comes to physical issues and 100 percent of the time when the physical issue is truly an emotional issue at the root of it.

It goes without saying that whatever physical issues you're working on, always seek medical attention and take good care of yourself. If you break your arm, you should probably stop tapping and go to the hospital. *BUT* . . . those feelings of panic on the way to the hospital, feelings about the broken arm or how you broke it, the fear of how much the medical bills for the hospital will be, and the physical pain can be supported quite a bit by tapping on the feelings and symptoms.

EFT and Physical Pain

Bonnie came to me after suffering from horrible migraine headaches for years.

"Absolutely, no way, for sure, there is no way EFT can help me with my migraines! I have had them for twenty years, and I saw a neurologist sooooo . . ." Bonnie said.

I smiled at her. "I understand. That must be so frustrating. Would you still be open to doing some tapping on the headaches?"

"Yes, please, I would love that," Bonnie said.

To begin, I asked a few crucial questions about the headaches. "When did they start? Was there something significant going on at that time in your life when they started? Is there a time of day that the headaches are worse or better? When you close your eyes and ask yourself if the headache had a color or a texture associated with it, what would it be?" After a few rounds of tapping (less than ten minutes), Bonnie reported that the headache was gone. This really freaked her out actually.

"You don't understand; I saw a neurologist for this."

Together we discovered that her headaches came on every time the weather switched from sunny to cloudy or rainy. We discovered that she blamed herself for the headaches because she was a really smart gal and should "have this figured out by now." All feelings that come up are important in the tapping process. Even if they seem small and silly, add them into your tapping script when tapping for physical issues on your own.

Protocol for Physical Issues

Tapping on physical issues can seem overwhelming at first, but I assure you that the very simple protocol I am about to share with you can have profound effects when tapping for yourself or with a loved one. Do not overcomplicate the following.

I invite you to think about tapping for physical issues as experimental. The great news is that you can never get worse with tapping; there are no adverse side effects or reactions. The worst thing that could happen is that the tapping does not work, and the best-case scenario could result in the freedom from pain, clear solutions to everyday issues, or simply having more energy. Sometimes if the pain does not go away, and there really is a need to seek a medical or healing professional, tapping can help clear the cloudy thinking and open the gateway to finding the right doctor or healing practitioner who can support you the best. For example, when I was dealing with knee pain, I tapped and tapped and tapped on the pain. The tapping helped with the pain, but it mostly helped with my feelings about the injury. I was frustrated that it wasn't getting better and sad that I could no longer do my favorite activities like hiking and practicing yoga. Once I was able to tap on the frustration and sadness, I could pay attention to my intuition better and was more open to divine guidance. I tapped and tapped for about an hour one day, and the very next day, three people recommended to me to see a certain foot reflexologist, who happened to be my friend's husband. I took this as a sign from the universe, which was probably there the whole time, but the emotions related to the injury were clouding my guidance. After two sessions with this foot reflexologist, my knee injury was history.

Protocol for tapping on physical issues:

1. First start tapping on the symptoms of the issue. I will use hip pain for this example. Write down specific symptoms of the hip pain. For example, hot, dull, sharp, stabbing, tight, grinding, twisty, wrenching, swollen, crackling, weak, inflamed. Do a complete round of tapping on just the symptoms. This may be enough for the pain to shift and release. Be sure to get a SUD level for the amount of pain, from 0 to 10. This is crucial so that we can tell if the tapping is working. Tapping for this example could sound like:

    [Setup statement] *"Even though I have this tight, hot, stabbing pain in my hip, I still deeply love and completely accept myself."*

    [Reminder phrases] *"This stabbing pain in my hip, all of this hot pain in my hip, this tightness I feel in my hip, I have been so uncomfortable, and so on."*

2. Next, write down any feelings about the hip pain. How do you feel about the pain? Examples include:

   - Frustration (*I want to do this activity but I can't*)

   - Anger (*my body is letting me down; this is not fair*)

   - Fear (*I may not be able to do the things I want to do anymore and might be losing something that I don't want to lose*)

   - Hopeless (*I have tried everything and I am not able to figure this out*)

   - Sad (*I am not able to do the things that bring joy*)

   - Embarrassment (*I should know how to fix this*)

   - Discouraged (*I should be making progress faster*)

Find the main emotion that you feel about the pain/injury and get the SUD level from 0 to 10.

3. Tapping for this example could sound like:

   [Setup statement] *"Even though I have this frustration about my hip pain, I still deeply love and completely accept myself."*

   [Reminder phrases] *"All of this frustration I feel, it is so frustrating that I am still dealing with this stabbing pain in my hip. I wish I could do the activities I love, but this pain is ruining all my fun; it is understandable that I have so much frustration."*

4. If the pain persists, go a bit deeper. Ask yourself the following questions: When did the problem start? What was going on in my life when the injury started? Is there a certain time of day that the pain is better or worse? Take a moment to do a self-assess-

ment to see if there is a pattern to the pain. Tapping for this example could sound like:

[Setup statement] *"Even though I have this remaining pain in my hip, and it starts every time I sit down at my desk to work in the evening, I still deeply love and completely accept myself."*

[Reminder phrases] *"This remaining pain that I feel, I feel it most evenings when I sit down to work, this pain in my hip when I am sitting too long, this started when I took this job in the evenings, I sit at my computer and read emails for hours and my hip starts hurting, this pain is so frustrating, and so on."*

5. Complete your tapping cycle. Time to check in. How is that hip pain now? Throughout this process keep measuring your SUD level to see if the pain is improving. If it is still there, go to step 4 and continue the process . . .

6. Time to look for metaphysical clues: inspired by the queen of affirmations herself, I turn to Louise Hay for guidance in this area, in her book *You Can Heal Your Life*.

    In her book, Louise explores the idea that physical issues may have an emotional root, and it is a wonderful resource for finding an affirmation to counter whatever problem might be manifesting as a result of such. For example, lower back pain may be a sign of not feeling supported, teeth clenching and throat/ jaw issues may be from not speaking your truth, knee pain or foot pain could be a fear of taking the next step or not knowing how to move forward, and a splitting headache could be a result of being torn in two different directions.

At this time in the physical issues protocol, ask yourself if there are any clues to be found. I keep Louise's book by my desk for every tapping session that I do and I refer to it often while working with my clients. I ask if they are interested in hearing a possible metaphorical interpretation. Symbolic or metaphysical clues may not resonate with you or someone you are working with, but when it does resonate, wow! They can be a game changer. Tapping for this example could sound like:

[Setup statement] *"Even though I have been holding this pain in my hip, and it feels like unexpressed resentment, I don't feel as supported in my relationships as I would like, I still deeply love and completely accept myself."*

[Reminder phrases] *"This remaining pain, this remaining frustration and resentment, I have been holding on to it in my hip, the truth is I do not feel very supported in my relationships, and I need more help than I am getting, everyone seems to take take take from me, and I need some extra love, I want to thank my body for communicating with me, and I want my body to know that I got the message, I am willing to get this message my body is trying to tell me, and leave my body out of this moving forward."*

Add in Colors & Textures

Another good question to ask when tapping on physical issues is: If this pain/issue had a color or texture associated with it, what would it be? This may be hard for some people to tune into, and for others, the color/texture will pop into their minds right away. For example, one of my clients, Moonie, wanted to work on tapping for creativity. So I asked her what was standing in the way of her creative energy that day? She said her neck hurt really bad, measuring a 6 out of 10, and the pain was distracting and zapping her energy.

I asked, "If this neck pain had a color or texture associated with it, what would it be?" She mentioned it was a deep red color and had a chalky sandpaper texture.

We tapped together:

[Setup statement] *"Even though I have all this pain in my neck, and it is distracting me from my creative flow, I still deeply love and completely accept myself."*

[Reminder phrases] *"This pain in my neck, this distracting pain in my neck, this deep red pain in my neck, this chalky sandpaper pain in my neck, all of this tightness in my neck, it is keeping me from my creative expression, and I would like to let go of whatever pain that I can today."*

The pain went down to a 3 out of a 10, and we could proceed with the session for creativity.

Chasing the Pain

Sometimes when tapping on a physical issue, the energy of the issue can shift. This is pretty wild to experience when it happens, especially if you are the one feeling the shift. This is essentially what we want, for the energy to shift and go away. But sometimes the energy will move throughout the body in a seemingly nonlogical way, and the best thing to do is to "chase the pain" and keep tapping on the symptoms and where the pain goes. One of my dear clients, Sasha, wanted to do some tapping on the pain she was feeling in her breast. We followed the recommended protocol: she was a 7 out of 10 pain, and was fearful that there was something really wrong with her breast. She was also angry with herself because she was working at a job she hated, and her health had been declining since she had started there eight months prior. "I wish I was brave enough to leave that job," she said.

We tapped and tapped on the breast pain, the fear, and the anger. As we were tapping she stopped and let me know that the pain had moved. It was now in her left breast instead of her right breast, and she apologized because of how weird that sounded. I knew this was actually a good sign, and let her know that we just continue to be persistent, chase the pain, and start again from the top.

> [Setup statement] *"Even though now I am feeling this pain in my right breast, and I have this remaining fear and anger, I am choosing to see this as a good thing. Maybe this breast pain really does have an emotional root if it is moving."*

> [Reminder phrases] *"This pain in my right breast, this pain seems to be shifting, so weird that it is in my right breast now, I am grateful to my body for communicating with me about this, and I am willing to get whatever lesson I can and get this distress out of my body. This remaining pain in my right breast."*

Sasha gave me another confused look. "Steph, this is so bizarre; it is back in my left breast now."

We just kept tapping and tapping and following the energy of the pain. The pain kept jumping back and forth for about ten minutes, and then a whole lot of emotion came out. Sasha looked like she was having an aha moment and said, "I think my breasts are pissed at me because I have been allowing my super mean boss to 'milk' me, my energy, and time, and I am tired of being treated like this!" After a big release of tears and expressing how she really felt about her boss and work situation, the pain was gone. We were both amazed. And I am happy to report that the breast pain never came back for Sasha.

Jamie

One of my dear friends, Jamie, had an opportunity to do some tapping in the Western medical world. For years she had struggled with her weight and high blood pressure. She went to the doctor and her blood pressure was very elevated. Her doctor was very blunt and did not sugarcoat his opinion to spare her feelings. He told her many times that she needed to lose weight and she knew a lecture was coming if her blood pressure reading was high that day.

After the nurse got her blood pressure number, Jamie's eyes got big. Oh no! "Um, Gloria, do you mind if I do a little EFT tapping and you could take my blood pressure again? I am trying to avoid a lecture from Dr. Wilde today if possible." Gloria said, "Excuse me, try what?" Jamie explained that EFT was a little trick that she had been learning about and it would only take a few minutes. Jamie had a stressful day coming into the doctor's appointment and her intuition was telling her it was worth a try.

Gloria gave Jamie the side-eye as she tapped on her body and said as softly as she could in a doctor's office, *"This high blood pressure, this high blood pressure, all of the pressure in my system, this stress from my day is probably contributing to this high blood pressure, I would love to come to a calm and peaceful place about this and allow this blood pressure to come down. Any stress I am feeling, any tension I am feeling, I am willing to let go of what I can now."*

Meanwhile, Gloria was not impressed. When Jamie finished, Gloria retook her blood pressure and found it had dropped from 160/90 to 120/80. They both looked at each other and simultaneously said, "Holy s***, it worked!" The nurse went on to ask her all kinds of questions about EFT before the doctor called Jamie in for her appointment.

Ruby

I met Ruby in my EFT Level 1 training. Her presence was powerful and graceful. I liked her immediately, and she laughed at all my jokes. She wore a headwrap on her head and had perfect flawless skin and a calming essence. On day two of the training, we were at the point where I started to introduce how EFT can help support our physical body. I asked if there were any brave volunteers who would like to be my client for the demonstration, and Ruby raised her hand. She told the group that all of her hair had fallen out nine years earlier. It actually all fell out when she was one year old, then grew back, and then would fall out from time to time in patches. It was all gone now, since 2012. You could hear the silence in the Zoom room: Everyone's eyes were locked in. I could almost hear the participants' thoughts say, "Tapping ain't gonna help this one, Steph." And I had that thought too. Her hair was unlikely to grow back in the next ten minutes. So I asked her that obvious but brilliant EFT question, "How do you know this is a problem?"

Keep in mind at this point in the training, everyone in the group knows each other pretty well, everyone has been practicing tapping together, they are familiar with my sense of humor and have been practicing getting brutally honest with what is wrong or perceived to be wrong in order to work on it. When you have ten to twenty minutes to practice a new thing, you don't want to waste time getting the whole back story, so the students learn to jump right in. Ruby was a natural at EFT and I knew she had a bit of a twisted sense of humor like me. She caught on very quickly and mentioned how much she enjoyed focusing on the negative aspects, and was kind of over how people try and be so positive all of the time.

She went on to tell us that she missed her hair; she wished she had it back. She said that this hair loss had been a problem because she had always stood out; she has always looked different. She felt embarrassed, ashamed, mystified, frustrated, and puzzled because she had not been able to figure it out. Because we had learned about secondary gain (*a subconscious reason for keeping the problem, I will talk about it in chapter seven when I talk about addiction*) earlier that day in the training, she shared there was an upside to this hair loss problem, and that was when people met her now they were nice to her. She said people assumed she was sick, and they saw her as a full person. This was a nice comparison to when she was younger, when she got teased about being Asian, wearing glasses, and not fitting in at all.

She let me know that the number one emotion she was experiencing was frustration because she had tried so many things, because it had been so long and nothing worked. She let me know that the frustration was about a 9 out of 10. She was sure it was impossible to heal. She said it is not easy looking different and feeling different.

We first started tapping on the frustration: *"Even though I have this chronic hair loss problem, and it is so frustrating, I still deeply love and completely accept myself."* We continued on: *"This frustration, this embarrassment, this has been so confusing. I have been struggling with this for so long. I don't even know who I would be without this hair loss problem.*

"Just in case my subconscious mind is preventing my body from growing this hair back, I am letting my body know it is OK. Perhaps part of me is afraid of being treated badly again. Even though I look different, I am choosing to know I am uniquely beautiful, and beau-

tifully unique. If any part of me is afraid to grow this hair back, I am willing to send that part of me love right now. This part of me could be keeping me safe, safe from being cruelly teased again. Even though I do not remember who I am with hair, I am willing to remember. I am choosing to know that I deserve to be treated like a human being, no matter if I have hair or not. Even though it feels like there must be something wrong with me, I am willing to consider that there may be nothing wrong with me." Then some playful, ridiculous tapping: *"Actually, I'm sure there are plenty of things wrong with me, my sick sense of humor being of them, and maybe it has nothing to do with my hair."* At this point, Ruby burst into laughter. *"I am actually an incredible human being, no matter how much hair is on my head, so I would love to let go of some of this frustration if I can. If only this frustration helped me grow more hair on my head, I would get more frustrated! But it is probably not helping me right now."* Validating her feelings, I prompted, *"This frustration makes so much sense because I have tried so many things. I am going to honor my frustration right now: anyone else would be frustrated if they were in my shoes."*

After tapping and tapping together, as the group observed, we took a pause to check in, drink some water, and check for progress. Ruby reported that her frustration was currently at a 0, and she did know how uniquely beautiful she was.

She even laughed a bit as she reported, "It never occurred to me that there was nothing wrong with me."

Using humor and laughter can be one of the biggest emotional releases with tapping. Keep in mind that humor does not always land or resonate. But because Ruby and I had a connection, I knew I could go there with her.

Nina

When the coronavirus hit in March 2020, people started heading online to find resources and support their mental health.

This included heading to YouTube to tap away the fear of getting the virus that was spreading across the world. After finding my tap-a-long video on letting go of fear, I had a client reach out to me from across the country. She already had the virus, so we did not need to tap on the fear of getting it because the worst-case scenario had already happened. So I asked her that obvious but brilliant EFT question, "Why is having this virus a problem for you?"

You see, this sounds like a dumb question, but in reality, there could be many different answers to this question. For example, one person might say they are afraid of the pain they will endure during the sickness, and another person may say they feel sad they may die without ever meeting and marrying the love of their life. Others might say they are disappointed thinking about passing away without ever being able to see their grandkids grow up. This is another reason it is so important to be specific with EFT; the more specific we get, the closer we can get to the root of the problem.

Nina let me know that she did not have a fear of dying. She said that she was a very spiritual person, and she knew she would find peace on the other side if she crossed over. But Nina had a ten-year-old son, and the fear of leaving him behind without a mother was a 10 out of 10 on the fear scale. This possibility was her worst nightmare as she lost her mom at a very young age and it was horribly traumatic for her. We tapped and tapped on the fear together. We decided to have a very short session because she was sick and would get tired very easily. Usually my sessions are ninety minutes, but we agreed that a forty-five-minute session would be our best bet. In that amount of time, after getting as much background as I could and tapping on all of the aspects of her fear, we were able to get her fear down to a 5 out of 10. The goal is usually to get the fear to a 0, but I felt a 5 was very successful.

If you think of two people with the same condition, and one of them is a 5 out of 10 fear, and the other is a 10 out of 10 fear, who do you think will heal faster? Probably the one who is a level 5 because you know what? It takes a lot of gosh-darn energy to be fearful. In this particular case, fear was the absolute worst symptom she was having. My concern for Nina was that fear would rob her body of its vitality and thus its ability to heal itself.

More Notes for Tapping for Physical Issues

The body is dense. When working on body stuff, there is no need to rush. Being patient and persistent is effective when working on physical issues, as they may take a little more time to clear. For example, if someone is tapping on jaw pain, it is unrealistic to say, "Hey, let's go into the jaw space and take out all of the stress in one go!" That might leave someone needing quite a bit of recovery time, and they may not be ready for that kind of release. Chipping away at the distress in the jaw, bit by bit, may be more effective and make it feel safer to approach.

Journaling exercise for tapping on the physical body:

- What is standing in the way of me feeling completely balanced and healthy in my body?

- If I get quiet and listen, are there any messages my body has been trying to tell me?

- Have I been judging my body? If so, why? What would it look like to have my body and me on the same team?

- If I could have a heart-to-heart with my body, what would I want to say?

- What am I grateful for about my body today?

6: Weight Loss

"And I said to my body softly, 'I want to be your friend.'
It took a long breath and replied, 'I have been waiting
my whole life for this.'"

—Nayyirah Waheed

I met my friend Alice in the office. We became fast friends in that small office and supported each other through the ups and downs of the corporate world. One day I came in and she was pacing back and forth murdering some words under her breath. "I can't believe the nerve of her; who does that? How can someone be so rude and act like this at work."

"Hey, girl, what did she do this time?" I asked.

I knew exactly where the problem was. We had an evil boss. She was so awful that sometimes we wondered if her full-time spiritual gig on this planet was meant for tormenting and sabotaging others. It made for a harsh working environment and a lot of spiritual growth. Alice was pissed on this day, and the evil one had gone too far about something.

"This may be an obvious question, but would you like to do some tapping with me?"

"Yes," she said, "but tapping probably won't help with this one: it is probably time for me to quit this job as I don't see this environment getting better with the evil queen in charge."

We decided it was worth a shot and tapped and tapped together for twenty minutes. I told her to just let it rip: no need to be politically correct, nice, or fair. And she did. We tapped through the feeling of dread of having to deal with the boss, feeling of anger at being spoken to with such a rude tone, and feeling of confusion because it seemed that no matter what she did, the office dictator was not happy. After about a week, we finally got a little time to chat alone in the office again. I whispered to Alice so I wouldn't alert the sleeping dragon on the other side of the office that any funny business was going on.

"Psst, hey . . . how have things been going since we did that tapping thing last week?"

She let me know that the work situation was a little better, that the evil queen seemed to have found something else to focus on so she wasn't getting as much criticism anymore. She let me know that the real tapping miracle actually had nothing to do with work.

"Every evening when I come home from work, I battle with a box of Girl Scout cookies, and I usually lose this battle. I justify eating one, and then I walk away, and then it is a back-and-forth self-negotiation and excuse-creating charade for the rest of the night. I white-knuckle the box and say, 'just one more,' at least ten times. But this last week, the cookie anxiety was gone. I didn't even think about the cookies or want the cookies. It was just suddenly, 'meh' no big deal. You don't understand, Steph. This is a huge deal! I am not sure what you did, but this is a little miracle for me."

Alice let me know that she had put on about sixty pounds in the last year and this was the first time the scale seemed to go the other direction since our tapping together.

Clearing up your emotional state is always the goal when tapping on anything physical, including weight loss. If you choose to use tapping to lose weight, think about it as if you are using tapping to lose your emotional weight, and when you are able to do that, the physical weight will balance out. Once we are at peace with ourselves and we have cleared up emotional disruptions, usually caused by the stress response, traumatic memories, and limiting beliefs, the body is free to come back to its natural balanced state, including letting go of extra weight it might be carrying around.

Tapping essentially is a tool that can help you unblock yourself, and unkink your garden hose, in a very real way. Kind of like a helpful garden expert neighbor coming over to help you get things set up properly, and take the time to unravel the hose, shake loose the stuck parts, test the flow of the water in the hose, so it doesn't need to work so hard anymore to do its thing. There is nothing actually wrong with the hose; the hose does not need to feel shame for getting twisted. It just comes along with the role of being a hose.

When it comes to weight issues and food, there is no way to really avoid it. We don't really get to take a break from having a body or just let our friends know, "I am not really doing the whole eating food thing right now so I will pass." We make food decisions multiple times a day, and the day will go by a lot smoother when we are not making decisions and consuming nutrients when we are feeling stress, anxiety, guilt, and having thoughts of calorie counting and a diet-culture narrative. Sometimes it is not about the food at all. Weight issues are often not an easy topic; there are usually layers of complexities and complications, and years of reinforcement. Consider yourself lucky if you have freed yourself from weight issues with a simple strategy. I have found in my practice that weight stuff takes about twelve sessions usually, while other topics will take about three to five sessions.

In this chapter we will cover ways tapping can help support emotional eating and food cravings, examples of the main obstacles tapping can help with when someone is struggling with weight, and how to come to a more loving view of your body. One caveat is that if you have bulimia or anorexia and are hoping to use tapping, you will want to have an absolutely dedicated medical team around you and not just do tapping on your own for your sole support.

Emotional Eating & Food Cravings

I want to start off here by mentioning that emotional eating and food cravings are completely natural and a great opportunity to notice what comes up when we do not have that food or substance. If you haven't noticed by now, when stuff comes up, it is uncomfortable, and eating is very much one of life's comforts. Remember the *F* in EFT stands for freedom, and the goal is to have freedom around the desire to eat that chocolate or consume any type of food. I would even argue that when we have more freedom around certain foods, we are able to enjoy them more! It is possible to be so tied up in all of the emotions around eating a certain food that it may be distracting us from the experience of actually enjoying it.

Tapping for food craving protocol:

1. We will use chocolate for this example, but in your head you can think of something that you crave and make this process specific to that food or substance. If this is a pretty serious craving or a bizarre craving, it might be wise to work with an experienced practitioner for this, but it is definitely worth a try on your own.

   Think about this food and give yourself a rating from 0 to 10 on how much you are craving the food at this moment. Even better, if you can grab a little piece of chocolate or goodie, hold it in your hands, take a whiff, and then measure from 0 to 10. Start by tapping on the actual craving itself, adding any descriptions and feelings that are there.

[Setup statement] *"Even though I have this craving for this gooey chocolate, and I want to gobble it up at this moment, I still deeply love and completely accept myself."*

[Reminder phrases] *"This gooey chocolatey chocolate, how I love chocolate, I have this craving for chocolate, this craving, this craving for something sweet that I have."*

2. Look for specific triggers for the craving like stress, time of day, emotions, and even identity. Perhaps the craving comes on every day at 3 p.m. and you want to crawl under your desk and take a nap but you are sure you will be fine if you have a little pick-me-up snack. Or maybe you are a sensible eater all day long, and then when you sit at home with your partner and zone out with some TV, the sweet, salty, crunchy snacks accompany you on the couch. Are you known to be the office chocoholic and your employees know to bring you a fancy organic chocolate bar to cheer you up? How could you dare jeopardize that identity by not craving this food? Take a moment to think about this and write down any insights you might have about a food craving you wrestle with. Here are some examples of tapping once you have more clues about the food cravings:

[Setup statement] *"Even though I have this craving for chocolate every day at three o'clock, and I want to tear apart the file cabinets at work looking for a chocolate treat, I still deeply love and completely accept myself."*

[Reminder phrases] *"This remaining craving, this happens every day at this time, chocolate in the afternoon is my ritual, I don't know what my life would be like without this chocolate, I need it, I do not want to give up this chocolate, it helps me, well I think it helps me? I have put on fifteen extra pounds this year, which has not really helped me actually. I forgive myself for having this craving; it is completely understandable."*

3. How is that craving doing now on a scale of 0 to 10? The next question to ask is what emotions are coming up, and is anything surfacing after tapping on the initial craving and behavior? When I ask you to notice feelings, this is not a judgment thing, just an opportunity for self-awareness. What comes up here is the gold that will help us get to the bottom of the issue. Was there a specific event that happened when the craving started, when the emotional eating started, or when extra body weight seemed to start sticking to you? Examples of what this might sound like:

    [Setup statement] *"Even though I have this remaining craving for chocolate, which started when my husband left me two years ago, I still deeply love and completely accept myself."*

    [Reminder phrases] *"This remaining craving for chocolate, chocolate is so comforting to me, this chocolate really helps with all of this disappointment I feel, chocolate would never leave me like my husband did, chocolate is always there for me when I need it, every day at three o'clock, chocolate is good old reliable, humans can be so disappointing, but not chocolate, chocolate gives me something to think about so I don't feel all of this loneliness I have been trying not to feel."*

I would like to make a note here that it is OK to not want to give up a food craving; it is OK to love chocolate dearly. I know I do! I am suggesting that you might love this food even more after tapping on the emotional components around it so you are able to enjoy it instead of inhaling it when you are anxious about something else. You can consume food with more joy and presence. I also want to note that when tapping we are communicating with the subconscious mind, and eliminating the kinks in the hose that you may not even be aware of. If memories or more aspects pop up while doing this work, please make a note of them in your tapping journal. There is also a playlist on my YouTube channel dedicated to weight loss if you would like to follow along with me and tap on chocolate cravings, emotional eating, or letting your body know it is safe to let go of the past and those pesky extra five pounds.

Limiting Beliefs That Get in the Way

With my degrees in health science and health education, I had the pleasure of teaching for another company's weight loss program. Every week at the group meeting I would listen to the emotional components of the participant's weight loss journey, celebrate the wins, and problem-solve the obstacles. I was fascinated to observe that many of the everyday struggles of the participants actually had nothing to do with the food. It really didn't matter how many calories were in a cup of black beans when it came down to it, especially if there was a limiting belief in the way of true success. I created a little twenty-one-day tap-a-long course with the information that I gathered listening to those hundreds of people who walked through that program together. In this process I created a format for all of my self-guided courses: Week one, tap through the emotional components. Week two, tap through the limiting beliefs. Week three, step into a happy, healthy mindset.

Even though we are working with the physical health realm, mindset and beliefs play a huge role in whether or not your efforts are successful. I have spoken to teenagers who weigh 120 pounds who believe they are hugely fat and obsess about every dimple in the mirror. I hear some clients and friends say they feel shame every single time they eat, every single time! Shame is a guest at the dinner table whether they are eating a salad or a bowl of ice cream. When I work with someone in this realm, they are usually consciously completely ready to drop some pounds, but as we know by now, a lot is lurking around in the subconscious that can be sabotaging success.

I lead a live group through my "Tapping for Weight Loss" program once a year, and I am humbled and in awe of the beauty of the group. These groups are mostly women, who are extremely loving and radiate beauty, jumping at the chance to support one another and cheer each other on. They have the ability to see the beauty in others with no problem, but when it comes to themselves, they have tunnel vision, are focused on their flaws, and are extremely hard on themselves. In this weight loss program, we hardly talk about what to eat at all, the pure intention is to unkink the hose of the body (*and perceptions of your body*) so it can live, exist, be nourished, relax, and burn fat effortlessly. The intention is to support the underlying emotional issue that causes the emotional eating, body shame, and unrealistic expectations in the first place.

Once you tap through the common emotions, such as anger, grief, frustration, sadness, and judgment, we get to take a good look at limiting beliefs. Here are some common ones from the program and beyond. Please give yourself a little self-assessment here. Have you ever felt like the below statements are true?

1. I hate my body.

2. Having a healthy body is for other people.

3. It is not safe for me to be a healthy body weight (something bad may have happened the last time I was attractive or healthy looking).

4. Someone is to blame for the state of my body.

5. Weight loss is complicated for me.

6. Food is comfort.

We will talk more about beliefs in chapter 13 and I will show you how to tap on these (or any beliefs we don't want anymore) in order to make them less true using the VOC (Validity of Cognition) scale. This scale is a little different from the SUD (Subjective Units of Distress/Discomfort) level scale we learned about in chapter 3, when we use a scale of 0 to 10 to measure the intensity of any given emotion. Zero meaning no intensity of emotion, and 10 being the highest intensity of emotion possible. This is important as it can be the single largest factor in why you may not be getting the results that you desire.

Eleven Pounds with Ella & Ivy

"That's it? What a bummer; only eleven pounds down is just not good enough." Ivy scoffed at the results after we tapped every morning for twenty-one days in a row. The self-loathing and self-judgment were so strong with her that I could barely get a word in edgewise.

"I am just so disgustingly fat."

I heard this nearly every morning when the Zoom window would open up and our eyes would meet for her early morning session. Sometimes I tried to squint my eyes to see if there was something I was missing? But she wasn't disgustingly fat. At five foot eleven, Ivy weighed in at 155 pounds. She had a wedding coming up in a month and had the goal of reaching 130 before the big day, all without changing any of her behavior.

Every day, I asked, "How are you feeling today? What is standing in the way of dropping this extra weight? Has anything shifted from yesterday?"

Ivy would then share her emotional state and of course, we would tap on anything she was up against that day. I saw her progress over the twenty-one days, as she talked about how she decided not to eat all four corndogs for lunch and stopped when she felt full at three. She would share how her pants were fitting better, and how now she had more energy to get to the gym after work, but still, she did not feel satisfied.

Ella and I did the same exact program together as I did with Ivy, except Ella showed up in person every day in my living room at 6 a.m. Even though she lived about eight minutes away, this was an impressive commitment, for twenty-one days in a row.

We had a little tracking sheet that she marked up every morning when she weighed herself. "I have never been so dedicated to anything in my life," she shared. "I am so proud of myself; this is a really big deal for me, Steph."

We tapped and tapped mostly on grief and sadness about how she let her body get to the state it was in. Many tears were shed, and it literally felt like pounds of grief were melting away.

Ella weighed in at 283 pounds and had been heavy for most of her life. She ate really healthy food most of the time but would tend to want to eat vegan cupcakes at night to comfort herself. She had experienced lots of trauma and abuse as a kid. A psychic once told her that she had been carrying trauma in her body from the moment she was born into this world. Many memories of her childhood popped up during our time together and we tapped through them. She started walking with her dog daily and practicing yoga almost every single day and started experimenting with new recipes. At the end of twenty-one days, she had lost eleven pounds and felt amazing. She said it was the first time she was able to keep off over eleven pounds in the last eleven years. These eleven pounds represented a huge shift for Ella.

I share this story to illustrate the point that how you perceive yourself matters a whole lot. How you perceive your body matters, and how you feel in your body matters. Two people can do the exact same program, get the exact same results, and have a completely different experience. Weight loss is a completely individual experience, and yet there are a lot of the same themes that we see over and over, wreaking havoc on our progress. Weight loss does not go down in a straight line; it looks more like a jagged line, like the stock market line on a graph, going up and down slightly every day. And hopefully, it keeps trending in the right direction. I also share this story to illustrate how important our belief system about ourselves and what is possible for us is.

Tapping for Self-Hatred

When working on weight issues, sometimes it boils down to a self-loathing issue. This is the good news and the bad news at the same time. The bad news is that self-hatred is rough, time-consuming, energy-sucking, and a complete waste of time. The good news is that there is a lot of room for improvement and *REFRAMING* the perceived problem as a potential solution.

If we are able to flip the situation on its head, especially for sensitive beings, we can see that on some level, whether it is consciously or unconsciously, your body may be faithfully serving you by keeping that extra body fat on. Body fat can be an insulation for sensitive people, a protective shield from being hurt again. Logically you may understand that you are the coolest guy or gal on the planet, but if there is a subconscious belief that you need to be perfect in order to be loved, that brutal self-critic will shut you down.

So what can we do about this? Meet that critic, use its own words as we tap, and get you and your body back on the same team. The fact of the matter is, self-hatred tapping sounds awful, and you would likely never say these words out loud to another human being (even though you have said them to yourself) but there is such a release on the other end, I would encourage anyone who struggles with this to give it a try. Those negative words do not belong in your body or in your self-talk narrative.

Side note about folks who struggle with body shame and a loud inner critic: In my experience, these people tend to be the most fabulous, wonderful, kind-hearted, genuine people I have ever met. The real assholes of the world do not seem to be hard on themselves at all. I find this a fascinating phenomenon, that I expand more on in chapter 8. If you are hard on yourself take note that you're probably a really big sweetheart and the only problem here is it you are being hard on yourself. So let's tap, tap, tap all that s*** away so you can be free because you deserve to enjoy how wonderful you are. I will cover more about this in chapter 8 when we talk about self-love.

An example of self-loathing tapping with protective reframe could be:

[Setup statement] *"Even though I hate myself for being so fat, I still deeply love and completely accept myself and my body, as best as I can right now."*

[Reminder phrases] *"This self-hatred, this disgust with myself, I am just so incredibly fat, and I feel ashamed of myself; I get upset every time I look in the mirror. Consciously I would like to let go of this extra weight, but subconsciously my body is holding on tight to the fat; maybe my subconscious has a good reason for keeping all of this extra fat. Even though I am ready to finally lose this extra weight, maybe my body has been faithfully serving me and protecting me by keeping it on. My body has been trying to protect me from stress, and I would love to come to a place of compassion for myself and for my body, as best as I can."*

If you are currently on a weight loss or positive body image journey, I hope this information encourages you and gives you hope. Again, the goal is to clear up our emotional state, and in turn, our bodies can come back into balance on their own.

Journaling exercise for tapping on weight loss:

- Does my body have a good reason to hold on to extra body fat? Is my body trying to protect me or keep me safe from anything?

- Do I believe that it is possible for me to have a healthy, happy body?

- Did I learn unhealthy eating habits and attitudes at a young age?

- If I had an amazing, loving relationship with my body, what would my life be like?

- What am I making this extra weight mean about my value?

7: Addiction

"Addicts are some of the most extraordinary people."

—Terces Engelhart

Four years ago, my nephew, who was only twenty-two, was killed by a drug overdose. I found myself scavenging around the kitchen, looking for something to eat or consume. Usually, this would be pretty easy in my kitchen, but I was at my parent's place, house-sitting for a couple of days so there was no food or wine available. But I searched the cabinets anyway. I felt myself getting more and more agitated as I could not find any wine or snacks. I needed something, I thought to myself. And then I stopped and remembered a self-inquiry tool that I had learned years prior. I sat down at the kitchen table and placed my hand on my solar plexus (right above the belly button, considered our power center) and asked myself, "What am I feeling that I am trying not to feel?"

The answer came right away. Deep sadness. I was able to do some tapping for myself, thank goodness, but I learned a lot at this moment. As I sat there in an empty house, I grieved my nephew's passing. It was completely natural that I was sad; it made sense that I was heartbroken, and it was completely understandable that I did not wish to sit in that discomfort at that time. It takes bravery to sit in your own discomfort.

We can use many things to numb our feelings: drugs, alcohol, food, online shopping, sex, and social media. This "pick your poison" automatic response is actually completely natural. We do need comfort. Drugs, alcohol, food, online shopping, sex, and social media are actually all forms of comfort. But it becomes a problem when we reach for that comfort over and over and over again, never really allowing ourselves to feel the discomfort, and instead trying to avoid it. We try to self-soothe with substances or behaviors that are actually hurting us. This behavior may even be successful for a while, but eventually, that cupcake, new sweater, or gin and tonic will leave us feeling much much worse, and with the same original feelings since we were just stuffing them down instead of feeling them and releasing them.

I would like to take this moment to emphasize that there is nothing wrong with you if you self-soothe. This is something we all need to do, and to some extent, it can be a healthy process. For example, meditation can be a healthy self-soothing activity. I have a theory that sensitive people may struggle with addiction more than others because they *feel* so much that it is overwhelming. They pick up other people's energy, stresses, and the anxiety of the collective as a whole, and it is very common and understandable that they would want to numb out and not feel all of that. It is understandable for sensitive people to desire to feel normal, steady, and calm. If you think about it, reaching for a substance in order to feel some relief from overstimulation is a brilliant survival mechanism. With tapping, we are able to shift this perspective on its head with a reframe. *"How smart of me to want to protect myself from this pain and anxiety I feel!"*

Susie

Susie was a health nut, a sweetheart, a high-achieving entrepreneur, and she believed she had a problem with wine. If you asked any of her friends or family, they would say that sure, Susie likes wine, but they would never think of her as having a problem. Susie would have about one or two glasses of wine every evening, but maybe not if she needed to wake up early or had a big event the following day.

I had been working with Susie on a variety of issues for a few months on the topics of abundance, family stress, and losing weight. Our appointment was at 9 a.m. in the morning on a Wednesday and she said she wanted to work on her alcohol problem. I, of course, asked her that wildly helpful EFT question we learned in chapter 3, "How do you know this is a problem?"

She went on to tell me that it was not a problem in the traditional way that most people may observe an alcohol problem: It wasn't affecting her work or her relationships or her health negatively. But these couple glasses of wine each night were taking up a whole lot of mental space in her mind. She felt shame because it felt like her big secret in the closet, embarrassment because she loved wine so much, and failure because she was unable to quit on her own. She let me know that there was a distinctly different feeling when she casually had a glass of wine with dinner than when she came home from work after a stressful day and *NEEDED* the wine—when she needed it to take the edge off from her day. She didn't have a problem with the glass of wine with dinner, but the wine she *NEEDED* bothered her and it was not enjoyable when it was a necessity. Her mind raced about other things, and she wasn't present for the experience of the wine.

Together we did some basic craving tapping. She had some wine in the house so I asked her if she could pour herself a glass, yes, even though it was still 9 a.m. on Wednesday morning. She did. I asked her to smell it and rate her craving for the wine on a scale of 0 to 10. She let me know that the craving was a 6 out of 10, even at 9 a.m. on a Wednesday morning. This fact made her embarrassment go through the roof. She said it smells like relaxation. So we started tap, tap, tapping:

> [Setup statement] *"Even though I have this craving for wine, I still deeply love and completely accept myself."*

[Reminder phrases] *"This craving for wine, this intense craving for wine, what I am clear on, is that I have a craving for relaxation. Relaxation is what I really want. Wine is just a vehicle to help me get there. So whether I decide to have a sip of wine or not, I would like to take all of this shame out of the equation. All of this embarrassment, all of these feelings of failure, it feels like this is a problem for me. Even though I hate needing this wine, and needing it takes the joy out of the experience, I would like to get to a calm and peaceful place where I do not judge myself about this anymore. All of this self-judgment, all of this self-criticism, sometimes I feel like there must be something wrong with me."*

[Reframe opportunity] *"Whether I have a problem with alcohol or not, I would like to honor my amazing problem-solving skills; maybe this wine is not so much an alcohol problem, but an alcohol solution to my stress and anxiety problem. How brilliant of me to find a creative way to deal with this stress. If I want a glass of wine in the future, I would like to be crystal clear on whether I want this wine for enjoyment, or in order to relax. I would like to get all of this shame out of my system, and there is nothing embarrassing about needing to relax. And I am open to new ways of feeling peace and relaxation."*

Secondary Gain

I share this story because it is a good opportunity to talk about *secondary gain*. Secondary gain is where the perceived problem is actually a solution to a different problem. Susie really had a stress and anxiety problem, and the wine was a solution to that problem. Secondary gain is usually difficult to spot if you are tapping by yourself, and much easier to notice if you have the loving mirror of an experienced practitioner to reflect this back to you.

A good question to ask if you think there may be some secondary gain is, "Is there an upside to this problem?" or "What am I feeling that I am trying not to feel?"

Secondary gain can manifest in all sorts of ways. If someone has a back injury, subconsciously they may not really want to heal their back because the back injury means that they will not have to report to work at the job they hate. Another person may be keeping on an extra thirty pounds because the last time they were at a healthy body weight, they got unwanted sexual attention. In this circumstance, their body and subconscious mind are protecting them from being hurt again. Another example of secondary gain is someone staying financially broke because then people will continue to help them and give to them. Subconsciously staying poor is a solution to the problem of feeling loved and taken care of. Secondary gain is usually deeply unconscious and the person is not aware that they are doing this.

Steps to start tapping on addiction:

1. Tap on the actual craving. On a scale of 0 to 10, how intense would you say this craving for a substance is? Do some simple tapping here: *"This craving, this craving, this intense craving for this substance."*

2. What feelings come up now? Write down what feelings come up. Is there a deeper reason why you need the substance? What is accomplished when having the substance? (For example, lower social anxiety, less physical body pain.)

3. Journal and tap on the *WHY* underneath the desire for the substance. (For example, I need this marijuana

because I hate being at work and it helps me get through the day.)

4. Reach out to work with a practitioner if this matter feels above your own personal awareness. There is nothing wrong with asking for help from a professional.

Aspects to tap on if you would like to work on addiction for yourself:

*   Does it feel safe to be successful in sobriety from this problem?

    [Example setup statement] *"Even though I am not sure it feels safe to be successful at this yet, I still deeply love and completely accept myself."*

*   Can I imagine my life without this problem?

    [Example setup statement] *"Even though I am not sure what my life would look like without this problem, I can't even imagine it; I still deeply love and completely accept myself."*

*   Without this substance, I may really need to deal with my feelings, which I prefer not to do.

    [Example setup statement] *"Even though I don't really want to deal with this problem, And all of the feelings underneath, I still deeply love and completely accept myself."*

*   I may not really be ready to let go of this substance

    [Example setup statement] *"Even though I am not really ready to let these cigarettes go, I still kinda need them*

*and want them right now; I still deeply love and com-
pletely accept myself."*

Alan

Alan had suffered from alcohol addiction for years and now he was successfully one year and three months sober. He decided to put himself out there romantically again and sign up for various dating sites. He met a girl he liked very much and they dated for about three months. He was happy and grateful to have some companionship, genuinely liked this woman, and could see a future with her.

One day her financial situation changed. She found out that she would not be getting the $3,000 a month she had been living off the last few years and she decided that she needed more of a sugar-daddy-type romantic partner. She decided that the nice, financially average Alan was not the right fit anymore. Alan was devastated, confused, but mostly angry. He had many feelings about being dumped, especially being dumped over something so superficial. He was a sensitive guy, tended to take things personally, and had a hard time shaking it off when his feelings were involved. He had no tools to deal with these feelings, besides old reliable whisky. He fell off of the sober wagon and began drinking again within a few days of the breakup. He also went on a spending spree buying expensive guitars, various stuff online, and even bought a car.

If you are living with an addiction and want to see if tapping is helpful, I encourage you to start tapping on your feelings right away. This can be very general tapping, and it does not need to be fancy. If Alan had the tools of tapping, he might have had a better chance of dealing with the emotional carnage of the break-up. I can't say with certainty that things would have worked out differently and he would have stayed sober. But the whisky in this story was the solution to the actual problem, which was his (understandable) anger.

I made a joke once with my sober friend saying that I was definitely addicted to yoga. She set me straight right away letting me know that something is considered an addiction when it takes over your life and you have no control over it. I do not mean to make light of this topic, but to offer this tool as a support to the work one might already be doing for their sobriety or goal of sobriety. In his earliest training programs Dr. Rodger Callahan said, "The true cause of addictions is anxiety—an uneasy feeling that is temporarily masked or tranquilized by some substance or behavior." I like this approach because it takes the shame and blame off of the person.

In the 1970s, American psychologist Dr. Bruce Alexander gave us a lot of insight into the world of addiction with his studies, one of them famously known as the Rat Park study. If you want to know more about this study and this topic of addiction, check out Johann Hari's TED talk, "Everything You Know About Addiction Is Wrong." Basically, rats were put in individual cages with two water bottle options in each cage. One contained regular water and one contained a bottle laced with cocaine or heroin. He saw that the rats would drink from the drug-laced bottles until they overdosed and died. Then he started to wonder if it was something about the environment that the rats lived in, or if the drugs were simply that addictive. To test this hypothesis, he put the rats in cages together, calling them "rat parks" and the rats were free to roam, play and have sex. He observed, quiet remarkably, that in this new setting of connection, the rats were not all that interested in the drug-laced water bottles. They drank from them from time to time, but they never drank from them obsessively and never overdosed. This information teaches us that the opposite of addiction is not sobriety; the opposite of addiction is connection. I happen to believe that this goes a bit further beyond community and can include connection to oneself, connection to a higher power, and social connection in community.

Journaling exercise for tapping on addiction:

- What am I feeling that I am trying not to feel? Is there a deeper truth that I am currently ignoring?

- Is there a substance I use or behavior in my life that I feel shame about? How do I know this behavior or substance is a problem?

- What experience would I like to have when I use this substance or do this behavior?

- Is there an upside to this problem? Do I think it is possible that I have any secondary gain?

- What emotions come up when I think about the topic of addiction?

8: Self-Love & Acceptance

"Knowing that we can be loved exactly as we are gives us all the best opportunity for growing into the healthiest people."

—Mr. Rogers

I have my dad's bushy eyebrows, and I get them waxed once a month. I have never been good at small talk, so I appreciate social situations where I can go into deep conversation quickly with a seemingly random stranger, and a body waxing studio is one of those places.

I remember walking into my favorite waxing salon embarrassed about the condition of my eyebrows. I think I even said something to the effect of, "They got out of control before I realized it."

My wax technician and I started talking about life, love, and how normal things like getting your eyebrows waxed were very exciting in post-COVID times. We got to talking and she asked me what I was up to that weekend. I was in the fifth and final weekend of a shamanic apprenticeship program, and I wasn't sure how to describe that.

"Um . . . I will be sending prayers up for myself, our Mother Earth, and our community this weekend with my soul sister buddies—how about you?"

I did not know at the time that she was not only the best wax technician in town, but she was also a sociology major, and she kept asking me questions.

She asked me, "What is the biggest takeaway from your spiritual studies? Particularly from this program you are completing?"

I shared with her that the biggest teaching for me was what I learned about sacred reciprocity, and how we can give back to our Mother Earth. I knew before that humans take, take, take from the earth, but it was eye-opening to see this from a different perspective, how this throws off our energetic vibrancy as a species, and I was learning techniques about how to give back to our planet in both sacred and practical ways.

I then asked her about the biggest takeaway from her waxing profession. She said she was amazed at how common it was for women to apologize about their bodies. "With the many things that can be waxed, you can imagine the conversations," she went on. There was constantly apologizing for having a body, the maintenance of those body parts, and sometimes the (mostly) women would be apologizing for even existing. She told me that when some women were getting a Brazilian wax, they would often apologize about their female genitalia being so ugly and comment how nobody would want them with all of that hair.

One girl was getting her armpits waxed. She said she had walked to the appointment and apologized profusely that she may have some beads of sweat on her armpits. All of this apologizing, all while paying good money and enduring the pain and discomfort of a beauty treatment, and *she* was apologizing. She said that often she would tell the women on her waxing table, "Hey, guess what: it's OK to have a body, it's OK to exist, it's OK to want a beauty treatment, it is OK to not want a beauty treatment, you can stop apologizing to me at least."

Hearing this struck me at my core, thinking about apologizing for having a body, thinking about these expectations to look a certain way, thinking about this epidemic of self-criticism, and thinking about how I would never apologize for my big bushy eyebrows again. This relationship with ourselves can be the sweetest love story or the most gruesome battle against ourselves.

Consider for a moment that the inner critic may have a good purpose. So often the kindest, most intelligent, loving people can suffer from the most self-judgment, self-hatred and the repetitive narrative of "not good enough." Sensitive people tend to feel this more, asking themselves, "Why am I like this?" In response they get harder on themselves for picking up other people's energy, feeling so much, and being so hyperaware, that they create a self-fulfilling cycle.

I hear my clients often tell me how hard it is to care so much. And I would honestly have to agree, caring a lot about the world and other people can really suck sometimes because your heart can break into a million pieces, multiple times a day. And at the same time, it is a much better option than being completely apathetic and not caring about anything or anyone.

When I ask someone what is keeping them from deeply loving and completely accepting themselves, they usually list a few things in their life that aren't perfect: I can't love myself until I am at my ideal body weight; I can't accept myself until I make a certain amount of money each year and own a home; I definitely can't love and accept myself when my apartment is this messy, the dishes aren't done and there is two weeks' worth of laundry to do.

Whatever form it takes in our mind and body, it usually comes down to three ideas:

1. I can't love myself unless I am perfect.
2. I should be better than this by now.
3. What is wrong with me?

You can ask anyone who has struggled with self-love; they are usually totally dumbfounded about why they haven't been able to figure this out yet. Because logically, they really know they are great! But what if this self-judgment actually has served a big important purpose in your life? It potentially keeps you safe from things like smoking ten packs of cigarettes a day because your inner critic says, "Gross, those things are disgusting!" and this self-judgment has perhaps helped you not eat the entire pint of ice cream in one sitting because your inner mean girl says, "Yikes, have some self-respect!"

Self-judgment may have helped you to stay out of trouble to some extent. Have you pushed through obstacles in the past because you knew you could be better? You can probably understand how the "not good enough" thinking has possibly pushed you to achieve a better quality of life in some respects, but for the most part, self-criticism is probably hurting you more than helping you.

Let's use this living situation as an example. Ben had lived in a small, crappy apartment for the last seven years, and he struggled to make a living. His dream was to own a home with lots of space. He wanted to have chickens and a big garden, but it always seemed just out of his reach with rising housing prices and his current salary.

This could go two ways: Ben could have a healthy goal to strive toward and visualize his dream house, with the challenge keeping him motivated to earn more, save more, and perhaps expand his search and think outside of the box. However, if Ben truly struggled with self-criticism, he would use this circumstance to beat himself up over and over, and let this situation be a vehicle to relive his *not-good-enough* story. See the difference? One option truly does not help him get closer to his goal but causes much more suffering and pain.

Every gardener has dealt with the un-fun part of caring for plants, and that is dealing with pests. Pests happen, whether it is bugs, caterpillars, snails, gophers, deer, or weird fungus you had to look up on Google. These things happen, and a gardener would never assume that it is somehow the plant's fault. The plant has nothing to feel ashamed about or beat up on itself about; these pests are just a part of plant living. We assume that it is the environment, the soil, and the placement and we think that there must be a creative solution to combat the pest situation, instead of relishing in the story of "that plant just doesn't have what it takes; it's just not good enough." Having an inner critic is just a part of human living, and I consider it a natural pest and nothing to feel ashamed about. Instead of hiding from the pest, or just watching it eat away at your budding bell peppers again and again, roll up those sleeves and take a good hard look at the pest. Let's shine a light on it, lay it out on the table and investigate that thing. If you are going to *off* this pest, you need to know what you are working with, especially if it is the biggest, ugliest slug you have ever seen. Put some gloves on if you have to and pry that thing off of your beautiful fruit and throw it in the trash.

When you are hard on yourself, you can talk and talk in circles. If that good, motivational part of being hard on yourself is not pushing you in a positive way, then no amount of being hard on yourself is going to be helpful. Tapping can help you not only end the repetitive loop of thinking, but it can also stop it in its tracks and make you laugh out loud about how ridiculous all of that negative self-talk sounds when it is spoken out loud.

You can't negatively talk yourself into a massive success, so let us try a different route. This is not an obnoxious, toxic positivity thing, quite the opposite. When we reviewed the principles of the process, we talked about how to focus on the negative. You really don't want to hold back when tapping on the self-critic, because you *do* want to get all of that junky stuff out of your system and out of your head. I mention this now because I do not want you to be afraid of focusing on the negative when tapping for self-love and acceptance.

Honestly, tapping on self-loathing, self-criticism, and self-hatred sounds incredibly brutal when you hear it. It really does sound awful to say all of those things out loud, as it is not something you would ever say to another human being. But someone can beat themselves up with it all day, every day. When working with clients struggling with this, I just ask them, "If your self-critic could have a free pass to *let it rip*, what would it be saying to you?"

Here is just a small sample of some real-life, self-bullying statements I have heard in a session:

- I am disgustingly fat. I look in the mirror and all I can see is my flabby, cellulite arms. I feel bad for people who have to look at me.

- I am the worst; I don't even want to spend time with me.

- I hate my voice. I hate my face. I hate my shoulders; I hate this gross mole on my neck. I hate my stomach. I hate this frown wrinkle on my forehead. I hate my big ass thighs that rub together when I walk and that don't fit into my pants anymore.

- I am douche-tastic.

- How could anyone ever love a face like this? I am painfully ugly.

- My body feels like a broken-down old horse, no one will want me now. I'm just too old and crotchety.

- I just sit there too shy to speak; it's mortifying to be around people.

- I feel worthless because no one wants to marry me.

- I am such an idiot for getting married.

- I am such an idiot for not getting married.

- I am a terrible mother, it's embarrassing and my kid knows I am full of shit when I say I am happy.

Do any of these sound familiar? I hope not, but if so, I have really good news for you. Instead of being stuck in this type of thinking, tapping can actually help. This is an example of a self-critic brain-dump list. When the same thought pattern is repeated over and over again, it creates a groove in your brain. Kind of like when water pours down the same path of rocks in a river over and over, it becomes the natural path, and it's tough to fight against that current when you want to change it. Tapping can break the cycle of this repetitive groove.

When I ask a client what they love about themselves, they often tilt their head to ponder the question, and it takes them a while to think of a few things to share. When I ask a version of the question above: 'Why does your inner mean girl think you are *not good enough*?' They do not hesitate and start rattling off a list of reasons because often that river path has been ingrained for a long time.

If you need to do some tapping on this topic yourself (and even if you don't, I would invite you to practice as an exercise), I'll ask you the same: What does that inner critic love to pick on you about? Make a bullet list of all the things it says: "Not smart enough, pretty enough, not a good enough athlete, and so on." And then walk yourself through the tapping process:

Steph's signature tapping process, specially designed to kick the inner critic's ass:

Step 1: Pause & feel. Stop and take this moment to pause and feel. Place one hand on your heart, and one hand on your belly, and ask yourself: "What am I feeling currently that I am trying not to feel?" Go within and listen.

Step 2: Write it down. Journal all of your feelings. Do not be polite or politically correct or nice; just go for it unapologetically, and get it all out on paper. And then, read what you wrote.

Step 3: Find the main emotion. There may be many emotions currently, but if you had to pick one main emotion that is front and center at this moment, what would it be? (Don't second-guess this part, you can always tap on the other emotions in the following rounds if need be.)

Step 4: Give that emotion a number from 0 to 10. How much are you feeling that frustration, sadness, or anger? (This may be difficult to put a number to, but just do your best. We are simply measuring to see if the tapping is effective.)

Step 5: Setup statement: "Even though I feel (fill in the blank with your main emotion) and (insert how you feel about yourself), I still deeply love and completely accept myself."

Step 6: Tap through the points and read your previous journaling out loud as you tap through them. Also, add any new thoughts and feelings that come up as you are tapping. Tap and tap and tap until you feel a shift of some kind, you run out of words, or it feels like a good time to stop.

Step 7: Pause & feel again. Remeasure that main emotion and see if there was a shift. Ask the question to yourself: Where is my number now on a scale of 0 of 10? And what is still there? Did the main emotion shift to a different emotion? Rinse and repeat this seven-step process as many times as you need.

Luna

Luna really wanted to be a mommy. She was thirty-nine and single, and she talked to her ex-girlfriend nearly every day. She was in her sixth and possibly final round of IVF (in vitro fertilization), which is a series of procedures that support fertility and the conception of a child. During IVF, mature eggs are gathered from ovaries and fertilized by sperm in a lab. Luna had one good, fertilized egg and was patiently waiting to see if the transfer was successful. This triggered many emotions and she was filled with anxiety about it being successful and about it not being successful, but mostly about waiting in the unknown. She had a fear that this could be her last chance and was partially already grieving the outcome and protecting herself from future disappointment by feeling indifferent. We tapped and tapped together on all of the aspects of her feelings and thoughts. Because her feelings were so protected deep down, we switched gears to what beliefs she had about this situation. (*I will go over tapping on beliefs in chapter 13, so this will be a little sample.*)

Luna had mentioned that somewhere inside her, she did not feel worthy of being a mom, so I asked her to raise her right hand and say this statement out loud: "*I am worthy of being a mom.*"

I then asked her, "How true is this statement for you on a scale of zero to one hundred percent? Zero means not true at all, and one hundred means it is absolutely true."

Luna closed her eyes and took a minute to check in. We found the emotion. She opened her eyes, now teary, and said that she was surprised that this only felt 20 percent true for her. When I asked why she mentioned that she thought maybe someone else would do a better job of being a mom, she was too old now, and the fact that she was doing the journey as a single person. She also noted that her house was too messy and disorderly. Additionally, Luna told me that she had a dream of meeting a little spirit who was to be her child. In the dream, the spirit presented as a ball of light and asked her if she was ready. The spirit said that it wants to be joyful and playful and was hesitant to come here with things being so serious all of the time.

We tapped and tapped some more:

[Setup statement] *"Even though part of me does not feel worthy of being a mom, and I am not sure I am worthy of this new baby spirit coming into my life, I still deeply love and completely accept myself."*

[Reminder phrases] *"I don't feel worthy of being a mommy; someone else can probably do it better. Part of me knows I would be an amazing mom, and any kid would be lucky to have me as a mom, and part of me feels too old and too single now. Part of me feels that my life is not orderly enough, and part of me feels that this opportunity to be a mom has passed. And I had this dream, and the spirit is not sure if they want to come here yet, even though I sure hope that they do. Even though it is so hard to be in this unknown space, and my mind can't think about anything else currently, I would like to come to a calm and peaceful place about this as best as I can. Even though I don't feel worthy yet, I would like to relax and know that I am way overqualified for this position. I would like to relax and embrace that joyful, playful energy that the new baby spirit was talking about. I would like to embrace this childlike energy now and create an even more loving space for new life. The fact that I even worry about being a good mom probably puts me way ahead of the game for being a mom. Even though this unknown is so uncomfortable, I would like to feel good about myself and about my life no matter what the outcome is here."*

We checked in again about the original statement: "*I am worthy of being a mommy,*" and Luna reported that she felt this statement was 80 percent true, and we both smiled. This is that magical moment when you know that a shift happened.

Reading this you might wonder what happened? What is different? When we tap on all of these thoughts and feelings, we are moving the rocks in the river bit by bit and disrupting the negative thought pattern that the water has been flowing through for so long. Sometimes this process is slower, moving small rocks, and sometimes, when we get lucky, a whole boulder will land in the middle of the river forcing a new flow of water to form. Why does this matter? If there were two women who were trying to conceive, and one believed that she was worthy of being a mom a little bit, and the other believed she was worthy of being a mom a lot, who do you think is most likely to be successful? Our thoughts are more powerful than we could ever imagine. The spiritual teacher and peace activist Peace Pilgrim said, "If we realized how powerful our thoughts are, we would never think a negative thought again."

Being a Sacred Witness / Sacred Mirror

A couple of years ago, I was doing my own soul work in a drum circle with my beloved friends. My intention that evening was to know my purpose here while on the planet and learn how I could best be of service while living this precious life. I was lying on the floor with an eye covering listening to the deep comforting sound of the drum for this shamanic journey, and Eagle Spirit came to me with a message. Eagle let me know that my duty, while I was here on earth, was to be a sacred witness. There was a reason I did not enjoy being front and center on stage. I love being around people who are expressive and completely themselves, but I actually enjoy being a sacred witness to them, holding space for them, and loving them. I learned that this is my purpose, my job, to see the beauty in others and remind them of it when they forget.

After that experience, I now have a theory that because some of the kindest, most beautiful, loving people on the planet can be so hard on themselves, they actually have a superpower of seeing the beauty in others easily. These *sensitive superhero* types have the ability to see the goodness in others instantly; they do not have to work hard to see it, or think to themselves, *Geez, how can I see the positive in this person?* They are people who tend to become therapists, healers, or who do any kind of one-on-one intimate work, and have a special purpose to be sacred witnesses. Not in a way that they do not participate in self-expression, but in a way that they are a reflection of the beauty in all of us. They just naturally see that essence in someone, even when that person is in their shadow, and in their darkness, they can see their divine beauty with compassion. They are natural sacred witnesses but can have the hardest time seeing their own beauty for the most part, or viewing their life with this same level of compassion. In contrast, the real *asshole people* (for lack of a better term) tend to be not all that hard on themselves. They think they are great! They have no real problems to work on. All while that inner critic of these loving beings is extremely strong.

I share this with you because I want you to give yourself a break if you struggle with an inner critic, and to know there is hope for quieting it down. When you are working on that inner critic and having a hard time seeing the beauty in yourself and of your life just how it is right now, I want you to consider that you might have another superpower altogether. You see the beauty in others effortlessly; therefore you may have the life purpose of being a sacred witness, and that does not mean that you are not enough.

One of my clients, Betty, was really struggling with her inner critic one day during our session, so I asked her if we could play around with this idea a bit. Betty is a brilliant and talented therapist who loves so big that she is often left feeling that she can never do enough and can't shake the looming sense of failure. I shared with her my theory of the sacred witness and she let me know that it resonated with her, that she knows without a doubt that is her superpower. I asked her to tune into her power of seeing the beauty in others, and then hold her right hand up, and turn the palm of her hand toward her. I let her know at any time she can hold up her hand and it can act as a sacred mirror, so that she can turn around all of that loving energy that goes out into the world, and gaze with those loving eyes back at her own reflection, and absorb all of that energy as self-love. She looked into her palm and burst into tears. She expressed that it was so confusing to her why she could not see herself in the same light and was struck by the amount of love that was possible if she turned her focus around. After a few weeks, Betty actually added this into her daily meditation and visualized all the love that she wanted to share turned around and aimed at her. It was not easy at first to see herself in this light, but she practiced receiving this reflection of the sacred mirror for herself daily, and saw results in viewing herself in a more positive way. She started tapping every morning and doing this visualization, and was able to see how far she had come and all that she was doing well instead or viewing herself as a failure. She was now a peaceful warrior in her mind instead of an imperfect work in progress.

<u>Journaling exercise for tapping on self-love & acceptance:</u>

- Do I have a loud inner critic? If so, what does it get on my case about?
- What does my inner mean girl really want?
- If I completely loved and accepted myself, what would my life look like?

- What are a few things I love about myself? And how would I like to show up better?

- What do I love about myself in this moment?

9: Relationships

*"Your task is not to seek for love, but merely
to seek and find all the barriers within yourself
that you have built against it."*

—Rumi

Do you ever wonder how some people end up together? And why do some people stay single forever? In this chapter we will talk about how you can use EFT to support your current relationships, find out how you may have attracted a certain personality type in the past, and learn how to upgrade your mindset to attract new love opportunities and enjoy more fully the one you currently have.

This is important for sensitive people as they are extremely loving and can often sense what their partner is feeling and needs, and tend to get their feelings hurt easily. Sensitive types care deeply about the people they love. They tend to long for authenticity, trust, meaning and depth if they are going to share their time with someone. They also tend to know that their own emotions can be overwhelming for others at times.

You can apply tapping to enhance your experience of romantic relationships, as well as use these principles for friendships, family relationships, and even professional partnerships. You can guide yourself through a few rounds of tapping from dealing with simple annoyances to significant relationship-changing big deals and experiencing other people in a more pleasant way in general.

According to Rob Nelson, my EFT mentor and friend, you can free yourself up to experience an entirely different reality in romantic relationships when you approach it in the quantum field.

You can find more about this theory in his book *Hacking Reality*. For now, I will walk you through this idea.

Take a moment to think about your life and the relationships you currently have in your life. We tend to think we are in a relationship with the same person all of the time. There are small mood variations from day-to-day, but for the most part, this is the same consistent person. However, multiple physicists believe that there may be multiple universes and many possible realities that are slightly different, one degree over, in these different parallel universes.

Essentially we can have different variations of this person we are in a relationship with, and our own energy affects how we observe them. Without diving too deeply into quantum mechanics, it's kind of like a *choose your own adventure* by cleaning up your own energy. If two realities are close to each other, they may be a little different, and if they are far away from each other, they are very different.

For example, I like to think about it in terms of Rob's phone scrolling metaphor. If you are in a relationship with me, there are different versions of me available. For instance, if you are scrolling through pictures on your phone, and there are multiple photos of you, you may appear differently from one photo to the next. You may see the whole spectrum from a looking great, going out to dinner in a new outfit image . . . to the I've been working from home all day and am still in my pajamas look. If you didn't know me, you could see one side of the spectrum and get a not-so-flattering version of Steph. You might assume that my jokes aren't funny and my insights are unexciting. And if you scroll all the way to one side, I even start smelling bad. You might think, yikes! This lady is awful! Then you start scrolling in the other direction, and I get better and better. My jokes are hilarious, my insights are brilliant, and I smell amazing. I get more and more wonderful. There are an infinite number of versions of Steph to experience.

The version of Steph that you get, the one you are in a relationship with right now, is the one that matches your vibrational weight. Out of all the possibilities available, you get the version of me that essentially matches what you have the ability to experience. In fact, the version of Steph each reader of this book is getting maybe a little different, even though you are all reading the same words.

How does this relate to tapping? What keeps any one person "stuck" with a version of a relationship or person that they don't particularly like is their resistance to it. If you have negative emotions about someone or everyday natural complaints about them: *"He's always telling dad jokes, he leaves wet towels on the floor, and it drives me crazy how much he plays video games,"* this is the version of them you will get. The negative emotions about those traits keep that person locked into that version of them, essentially keeping you both stuck in that reality. This is the charge in the electromagnet that we talked about in chapter 2 . . . as soon as you tap the emotional charge away around these traits, you have the opportunity to swipe right and get a different version of your partner, friend, or family member.

If you have ever made a list of what you would like to attract in an ideal partner, it might include things like kind, generous, good looking, brings out the best in me, and brings me soup when I am sick. We have a logical "wish list" from the conscious mind. But the tricky thing is that the subconscious mind has its own list, and this list is rather different. This subconscious list is written in invisible ink and it does not give a hoot about you being happy; all it cares about is reenacting trauma, and healing those parts of you that felt neglected, hurt, and unimportant as a kid.

Let's say there is a lineup of fifteen potential suitors. And in this example, fifteen guys are up against a wall like a police lineup. One of them, let's call him Joe, may appear to have a spotlight above his head; there is an excitement when you look at him. Oh my goodness, he could be the one! That excitement is the excitement of danger or the excitement of reenactment. Your subconscious is selecting them to play the role of the unavailable dad, or the mom who was a bully. There is another guy in this lineup as well, Dave. Dave may be standing there with a box of chocolates, a bouquet of flowers, absolutely adores you, and has a great job. He would make a fantastic father, but he is *BORING*. Dave is not exciting at all because he does not give your subconscious mind the excitement of danger.

I see this scenario over and over again in my practice. My client will say, "I saw Dave on Facebook; he was on vacation with his family. He is a surgeon and a devoted father now. Why did I not want him? I turned him down and chose this other guy who is completely emotionally unavailable, flirts with other women in front of me, and whom I have been supporting financially for the last eight years."

This feels like a selection error, because we have our conscious list of desired traits we were asking for in a partner. But maybe this selection process is freakishly accurate, attracting the very person who will help you work through the mom or dad issues that are still unresolved from childhood or in order to reenact a particular trauma. Our younger self who experienced the trauma desperately wants to heal, so it tries to recreate the same scenario in order to heal the past issue, remaining stuck in the same cycle and attracting the same type of personality over and over again. This is clear in hindsight of course.

The good news is if we are able to go in and clean up our emotional state, traumatic memories, and our limiting beliefs around relationships so that we may be free of them, we do not need to reenact them or recreate them anymore. We do not need to keep dating the same unavailable guy because Dad was never there, or keep working at jobs with a controlling boss because Mom was so mean to you. It is entirely possible to create something new, even make a quantum leap to a new dimension of existence.

If you would like to work on relationships, there are three main ways to approach it:

1. Tapping on your own feelings and beliefs about relationships (and how you are in relationships) and what is possible for you. If memories pop up when exploring this, it is best to make a list of these memories and bring them to an experienced EFT practitioner. Give each memory a simple title, so they are easy to reference. For example, "Thomas cheating story." You can do a lot of amazing work on your own, however, with the tapping protocol below. If you are single and looking for a relationship, I recommend that you commit to this tapping work for at least twelve sessions with an experienced practitioner, before putting yourself out there. We want this because the goal is to create a new different experience, not the same experiences you have been having.

2. If you are already in a relationship (romantic, friendship, professional), make a list and tap on all of the things that bother you about that person. Tap on any "problems" in the relationship and the emotional charge that go along with these issues. This will be helpful for a relationship that you want to continue. But also keep in mind that when we clean up our energetic junk, and no longer have the need to reenact trauma, the best possible outcome and highest healing for the relationship could also mean breaking up.

3. Breakups and tapping on heartache feelings: If you are going through a breakup or any version of heartache, first of all, I am so sorry to hear it. Breakups totally suck, any way you slice it. Know that true heartache takes a while to pass. And others, no matter how much they would like to help, may just not be able to say the right thing to make you feel better. So many emotions can come up in the tender months after a breakup: grief, sadness, anger, confusion, loneliness, guilt, frustration, despair, among others. Tapping can help to take the edge off the intensity and create a sense of lightness. Even if it is not all better, it can help you come back to yourself, and regain your energy for you again. I would also couple tapping with many other self-care activities.

Tapping for Yourself

When tapping for yourself in the area of love, I like to break it down into three main components: clearing out the past and limiting beliefs, supporting the current moment by removing energetic blocks and forgiveness, and then creating a loving mindset and presence. You can find this demonstrated in my twenty-one-day tap-a-long course on the DailyOM, *From Heartbreak to Soulmate with the Magic of Tapping*. Below is an example of the layout and topics of the course, and at the time this book was published, you can purchase the course for just $19 on DailyOM.com.

Week 1: Clearing out the Past and Limiting Beliefs

1. Being lovable
2. It should have worked out by now
3. Not attractive or successful enough
4. Broken heart

5. Unrealistic expectations

6. Fear of rejection

7. Letting go of past lovers

Week 2: Removing Blocks and Forgiveness

1. A fear I will never find someone

2. Loneliness

3. Frustration and impatience

4. I'm too picky

5. Dating is hard

6. All the eligible partners are taken

7. It is safer to stay single

Week 3: True-Love Mindset

1. I am self-love and self-care

2. My true love exists and is already out there!

3. Making space for love in my life

4. Sticking to my non-negotiables

5. I am grateful in advance for my love

6. Connecting with true love, feeling as though I have this love now

7. I have confidence in my path

Some of these topics may resonate with you, and some may not. As you read the above lists, does one particular topic stand out to you? I wanted to give you a couple of examples in order to get the juices flowing. Think about your own struggles with romantic love and journal for the following questions in order to make your own tapping script and follow the self-tapping process below.

Self-Guided Tapping Process

Step 1: Pause & Feel. Write down the thoughts, feelings and emotions you have about love and relationships. This can be any romantic relationship, friendship, professional relationship, neighbor, and so on. Write down all your feelings about this person, their actions, what you love about them and what bothers the heck out of you about them. This is not the time to be shy; this is the time to be as truthful as possible with yourself. There is no judgment here or need to play it cool. This journaling is just for you and your tapping script; you won't be showing this to anyone. Tapping is the time to be uncool and feel what emotions are there, even if they are not fair or justified, and especially if they make no sense.

For example, Mia is tapping on the following topic: "I am forty-five, and I am pissed that my boyfriend hasn't proposed marriage yet because my clock is ticking, and it is now or never." Mia may hold this inside of her at a casual dinner party with friends, but not here in the tapping space. We want to get all of those feelings flowing and uncover the emotions so they can get some air.

Step 2: Ask yourself, what beliefs do you have about love and relationships that do not serve you or that you don't want to have anymore? A good clue is to think about what you know about the harsh truth of life in relationships. For Mia's example, she would just like to be present and enjoy her relationship instead of having marriage and babies in the back of her mind all of the time. Her belief is, "It's too late for me." Here are some examples of limiting beliefs about relationships:

- Even if I am happy in a partnership, it will eventually go south

- I am just not good at relationships

- There are no more quality people left out there

- If someone really gets to know me, they won't love me

- Love hurts

- I am too broken to be loved

Here are some more self-inquiry journaling questions; answering these are a way to gain more insights into what beliefs are:

- How do I feel about my love life?

- Do I believe romantic love is possible for me?

- What has gone wrong in my past relationships?

- Is there a relationship pattern I can notice if I reflect?

- What is standing in the way of being fully present while I prepare for my next relationship?

Step 3: Now that you have your thoughts and feelings out on paper, take a look and read it. See if you can find the main emotion that you feel and measure it on a scale of 0 to 10. You can also measure how true the belief is you have about the relationship using the VOC, Validity of Cognition, measuring how true it is on a scale of 0¬–100 percent. For example, Mia is 7 out of 10 sad, and the belief that "it is too late for me" feels 80 percent true on the VOC scale.

Step 4: Setup statement: "Even though I have this sadness, because I feel that it is too late for me to get the things that I want in my relationship, I still deeply love and completely accept myself."

Step 5: Tap through the points: read everything you wrote out loud from your journal and tap through the points.

Step 6: Pause & feel. Remeasure that main emotion and see if there was a shift. Ask the question to yourself: Where is my number now on a scale of 0 to 10? And what is still there? Did the main emotion shift to a different emotion? Rinse and repeat this process as many times as you need.

Rosemary

Rosemary was a sweetheart, a talented massage therapist, and quickly approaching forty years of age. She had been with her ex for ten years, and now had been single for the last four years. At the time we met, we would often start conversations with, "So, are you dating anyone?" Which would usually follow with a groan reply of, "Naaahhh."

One day, we met up for a cup of tea on a sunny fall morning, out in front of a local coffee shop. The leaves were starting to turn color and it was great to see her smiling face and catch up on life. When the conversation circled back to dating like it usually did, Rosemary's smile turned into a big eye roll.

"Girl, I am so over it. If I have a soul mate, I want to know what the heck is taking him so long?"

I had shared with her that I had just learned this cool tapping tool and had been experimenting with tapping for love. For myself at the time, that looked like tapping on old feelings of heartbreak, fear of abandonment, and also being annoyed with the process of dating.

At the time, I was also a new tapping practitioner, and was practically begging people to tap with me because I wanted to practice as much as possible. Rosemary said she was totally down to do some tapping, even though we were sitting out in front of the coffee shop with plenty of people sitting and walking nearby. She was not pained about being single, but she reported that the main thing she was feeling was confusion and she was tired of doing life events by herself. We must have looked pretty weird tapping on our heads and bodies out in the open like that, but we went for it anyway.

[Setup statement] *"Even though I have all of this con-fusion, where the heck is my soul mate already, and he is sure taking his sweet time to find me, I still deeply love and completely accept myself."*

[Reminder phrases] *"All of this confusion, where the heck is he? I am doing pretty great on my own, but it would sure be nice to have someone to do fun things with. Where the heck is he? All of this confusion, it seems like he should be here already. Well I guess technically he is here on earth, but I haven't met him yet. He already exists; we just haven't crossed paths yet. Part of me feels like I will never meet him, and part of me has some hope that I could meet him very soon. I technically could meet him by the end of the day today, I could run into him at the grocery store, and he could drive up in his car right now."*

Right then, a car skidded up right behind her in the only free parking spot on the street. We both turned to see the commotion and saw a man get out of the car who was definitely not her soul mate. He was about eighty-five and dressed in purple from head to toe. We looked at each other and both burst into laughter. I shrugged my shoulders and said, "Welp, tapping works most of the time, but maybe not every time. I am still learning."

After the tapping-sample coffee date, this experience slipped my mind for a while. A side note here, tapping may not work every time, say what! In chapter 13, I will talk more about what to do if tapping does not seem to be working and I will give you some tools for troubleshooting the process. The wonderful part is that tapping cannot hurt or cause harm. By tapping for love for Rosemary, we are not somehow blocking her soul mate from finding her; there are no adverse side effects, except for possibly *wasting* ten minutes or so.

Two months later, I ran into Rosemary again at an event. She ran up to me, squeezed my arms, looked at me wide-eyed, and said, "Holy crap, girl, that tapping we did worked!" She reported that she was dating a very handsome musician, who also had a stable job (this was on her wish list). She said she met him the very next day at a Halloween party and they have been all schmoopy for each other ever since. Rosemary and her now husband, have two adorable dogs and are very happy together.

Simon

Simon has been my friend for years. When you are friends with someone long enough, you get to witness their whole timeline of dating history. And you get to see how their relationships impact that person's life. When Simon met Grace, I knew he was in love. Not only was it a true romance, but it was also as if he was in a blast-off mode to personal growth and a success mindset. It was inspiring. He seemed so happy with Grace. She was teaching him a lot about making money, life, and thinking outside of the box. He was a water-ski instructor making $25,000 a year and feeling lost when he met her, and then two years later he was making well over $100,000 a year as an Internet marketer and working with her almost every day. And that is why I was surprised when he said things were not going to work out with her. He said he was hesitant, he wasn't totally 100 percent sure about her, and he wasn't really all-in like she wanted him to be.

"She is older. She has a couple of kids; I just don't know if I am ready for all of that," he shared. A few months after Simon broke up with her, she met a farmer down the road from where she was living who quickly became her new boyfriend. She had moved on, and life goes on too, right? But not so much.

"I can't believe she moved on so quickly," Simon said in disbelief. He was devastated. He was shocked. And they worked together every day, and Grace seemed totally fine.

"It's not that I wish she was suffering, well, maybe suffering just a little I guess?" During our session, Simon realized that even though he was on the fence about the relationship and ended the romance, he was devastated that she had moved on and was seemingly healthy, happy, and totally fine without him. He was heartbroken and she was fine. Breakups suck, it is just a fact of life, and EFT can help us get out of the emotional "take it personal" phase, and find ourselves again, our single, content, and ready-to-mingle selves.

Another aspect of tapping is exaggeration. What you want to do is say things so outlandish that you have to see the absurdity in it and break the connection of seriousness. So I threw in some extra bits that were over the top for our tapping session together.

> [Setup statement] *"Even though I am so hurt that Grace has moved on so quickly, I still deeply love and completely accept myself."*

> [Reminder phrases] *"All of this hurt I feel. All of this pain. All of this heartache. I can't believe she moved on. I can't believe she doesn't care. I broke it off with her, because I wasn't really sure, but now she has a new boyfriend. Ouch. Damn this hurts. How could she? It should take her a lot longer to move on. She should be heartbroken about me; she should be curled up on the floor in a fetal position crying for at least a couple of months."*

Simon burst into laughter because he could hear how ridiculous that sounded. He was able to break the connection between hurt and seriousness, and get some space to see the situation with his logical mind. He told me after that he really wasn't sure about her for the long term, and he had even more respect for her for handling the breakup with so much *grace* because she was still so kind and professional in the office.

Three weeks later Simon and I had our next session. I asked him how things were going with Grace. He looked confused. I said, "You know, how is that heartache of yours healing? How are things with Grace at work?"

He said, "Oooohhhh yea, oh yeah, that is fine, no heartbreak. In fact, I have gone on a few dates with a really nice girl from my AA group."

Just a few weeks later, I was not surprised to hear him say, "Grace who?"

There are lots of ways we can keep ourselves safe in relationships like overworking and being too busy for fear of intimacy, always finding unavailable partners because we are not truly available either, or even having crazy high expectations of someone so that they will always be set up to disappoint you so you can say, "Yep, told you, all of the good ones are gone and I will be alone forever."

In the garden, what you nurture will grow. What you water, what you tend to, and give attention to, will start to bud and create life. The same works for our thoughts, creating our reality. If you can tap away the negative thoughts, beliefs, and attitudes about love and relationships, success is inevitable.

And just a warning, or perhaps a heads-up, that strange things can happen when we tap for love/relationships. I honestly cannot even count the number of times that someone calls or texts while I am tapping about them. I have heard this many times from my clients too: "My exes just came out of the woodwork this week texting me and asking me to hang out." Also, after tapping with another client about her mom, she reported, "You won't believe it but my mom texted me out of the blue at the end of our session to say *I love you*." My client let me know this was out of character for her mom.

So don't be scared; give it a try! Tap, tap, tap on all of those aspects of the relationship for you and see what happens. You are worthy and deserving of giving and receiving love and being fulfilled in all of your relationships.

Journaling exercise for tapping on relationships:

- Do I have healthy relationships in my life?

- Do I attract relationships similar to those I have had with my parents?

- Do I have big expectations of myself or others in my relationships?

- How do I feel about love and romance, friendships, and family?

- If there were one relationship that I would have preferred to skip in my life, it would be with . . .

10: Prosperity & Abundance

"The universe is limitless, abundant, and
strangely accommodating."

—Pam Grout

There I was, eager to help with my laptop, ready and willing to be a customer service superhero. Before I was an EFT superstar, I tried out every type of career, in every field that you can imagine. I am not exaggerating. I heard, "Wait, what job are you doing now?" for years and years. I couldn't seem to make a living doing what I loved for many years; therefore I did every other job imaginable, that I didn't love, in order to pay the bills.

I worked in the ski industry, the auto industry, the senior care industry, the fitness industry, the medical industry, and the financial industry. I even sold car windshields over the phone at one point. I am not kidding; my job was to call people on the phone, all day, and ask them if their windshield had a crack in it. And hopefully, if it did, I would forward the call to my manager to close the deal and send out a brand-new windshield to be installed on the car in their driveway. I imagine if there was a prize for the weirdest and most random nonsensical career path, I would be a gold medalist.

At one particular job, which I loved actually, I was the behind-the-scenes administrative girl at an all-women's fitness gym. I made sure the coffee was prepped for the 5 a.m. class, I wrote the daily workout routine in big colorful chalk on the wall, and I fixed billing issues if there was a problem with someone's membership.

One morning the oldest woman in the gym came in for a workout. I automatically loved her because she was seventy-five and ran circles around all of the other women ranging from eighteen to sixty years old. She was full of energy and came to the gym ready to kick everyone's ass at Burpee Bingo. She wasn't so great with technology, however, and needed some help updating her credit card, and I was the gal who could help her with that. She bounced up to the desk and let me know she was having trouble with her account. I was excited to help because I knew how to do this task and it would be easy peasy. I just needed her name to look her up in the system.

I started to say, "What is your last name so I can look you up?" but I could only get in . . . "Whaaa."

She started on a long complaining rant. "Your system is too hard. It asked for my password and then locked me out. Damn it, how am I supposed to know my card is expired. I can't even go to the dry cleaners because my old card is saved everywhere."

I tried again: "Whaaaa." If I only had her name, I could fix it in about one minute. But the rant went on and on, twenty minutes of complaints. Something about getting charged, and then not charged, and then charged, and refunded, and how she emailed and called and she had the wrong phone number. On and on.

I had an aha moment with dear Polly, as I eventually learned her name. This is how the universe acts when it is ready and willing to help us. It knows what to do, quickly, efficiently, and with love; all we need to do is say the word and *ASK* for help. But there is another step: to shut up and listen for the guidance that we are passionately asking for. We are often so caught up in our own repetitive story, in our own compliant narrative, that the universe doesn't have a chance to do its thing, because we are blocking it. If Polly had taken a moment to work with me, we would have gleefully been on the other side of this perceived problem within minutes. But instead, the suffering endured longer.

The universe wholeheartedly is elated with the idea of supporting you in every way, including financially. With EFT, you can tap away that long complaining story about money and finances that you have perhaps been telling yourself for years, and step into a whole new financial reality.

Whether we like it or not, money touches most parts of our lives all day long. From managing our bank accounts on our phones to buying food, paying for a roof over our head, to supplying the simple necessities for life as a human. I know the Beatles sing, *"Money can't buy you love,"* but money can put gas in your car so you can visit your friends, pay for continuing education, buy new running shoes to support your fitness dreams, and so on. Even if you are not too much into consuming *stuff*, money can pay for self-care of all kinds like getting a babysitter, a massage, or a nutritious meal when you don't feel like cooking. In short, you may run into some trouble and experience loads of stress if you do not have a good relationship with money.

Whether you realize it or not, you have a relationship with money. Take a moment to consider your current relationships. How you feel about any given person (including yourself) is a big factor in how that relationship may be going. Money works the same way. Consider for a moment how you feel about money? If it feels like a bad word or awkward to even talk about, there may be some tapping to do on this topic.

If you are harboring feelings about how rich people are all greedy snobs, then your subconscious wants to protect you from becoming rich so that you don't turn into one of those *rich snobby* people. If you are able to see how stories have blocked you in the past, name them, tap on them, then you may be free of them. That repetitive complaining, poor-me story, can take a break for a while so the universe can guide you, give to you, and offer loving nudges in the right direction.

We have all known people who struggle constantly with money, and others who seem to flourish financially no matter what they do. Let's talk about why that is. No one intends to be stuck in poverty consciousness, the opposite of an abundance mindset. Some may have overheard stressed parents having arguments about money, or heard some kind of authority figure (parents, grandparents, teachers, coaches, religious figures, peers, television) say something along the lines of, "Money doesn't grow on trees" or "You have to work hard to make money."

These belief systems are often passed down to us unconsciously, and we have adopted them for ourselves without realizing. This only becomes a problem if the belief we have claimed as our truth is just *how it is* and is contributing to our poverty consciousness.

Money & Business Beliefs

I have had an entrepreneurial spirit since I was a kid. I think I was six years old when I opened a shop to sell my artwork. Obviously I was only six, which is not old enough to have a shop, but I had a fully functioning art gallery in my mind. I would make little drawings, watercolor pictures, and paintings, all on little 4x4-inch pieces of art paper.

I had one of those old-school, elementary school classroom desks in my room, and one day I decided to wedge the desk in the doorway to my bedroom. The desk was a perfect fit in the doorway, and therefore I was delighted to have my first storefront ever. I spread out the pictures on the desk in a nice display and added the price tag of ten cents on each piece of art. And then I sat, and waited, smiling from ear to ear, ready for a customer to walk by. Keep in mind, I was in my family's home, out in the country, and there were only six potential customers available. My mom, my dad, my brother, my grandfather, and my grandfather's friend Harry. We lived on a ranch and my grandfather and Harry were at the ranch daily to tend to the chores like feeding the cows and chickens, and irrigating the land. And maybe we would have some surprise visitors that day as well?

The next thing I knew, my brother walked down the hallway and glared at me. "What in the world are you doing?" he said with disgust in his voice. "No one is going to buy your stupid art, Stephie."

I didn't know it at the time, but I went into a freeze response at this moment, and I made a decision. Because my brother was obviously bigger and smarter than I was, he must have known something I didn't. You see, failure had never occurred to that younger version of me. She was a confident artist and joyful entrepreneur.

Usually when kids go into a freeze response, they make one of two decisions at that moment: There must be something wrong with me, or the world is a very scary place to be. This decision happens because they are doing their best to make sense of the world, and the more perceived survival value the belief has, the more deeply ingrained it becomes in our psyche.

When I was deep diving into my own personal work while learning EFT as a practitioner, I was also receiving sessions as a client. I recommend that all EFT students do this as well. We must do our own work so we do not bring our own emotional baggage into sessions with us. We only wish to be a sacred mirror, emotional support, and help others get distress out of their system.

This *brother* memory popped up during a session of mine when I was the client, and it was a huge *aha, whoa-Nelly, holy-moly* situation. I was able to see, plain as day, where this limiting belief had come from. I had decided at that moment that my brother was right, that no one would want to buy my art, and that it may have been foolish for me to even try. Luckily, I was working with a very skilled practitioner who was also trained in Matrix Reimprinting / Hacking Reality, and we were able to go into my memory and essentially do some tapping on my younger self that made the decision and created the limiting belief. This is an advanced tapping technique that requires additional training.

You may pursue this after earning your EFT tapping certification. If you are curious about Matrix Reimprinting / Hacking Reality, I will talk about it a bit more in chapter 15.

We were able to do some tapping with little Steph:

[Setup statement] *"Even though your brother just gave you some startling news, that no one will want to buy your art, you are still an amazing and smart little girl, and a very skilled artist. How clever of you to want to sell your art."*

[Reminder phrases] *"All of this shock you feel, it never occurred to you that you wouldn't have customers galore, the embarrassment that you feel, even though you think your brother is right about this, I have some really good news for you, your brother is actually wrong about this one. When you grow up, you will be just as artistic as you are now, and you will turn into quite the businesswoman. In fact, this is a very important moment for you, when you decide whether you will be successful or not, so now is a really good time to know that your brother is full of it. He may just be jealous of you because you are such a talented artist, either way, you have every right to be successful, and you have every right to be a joyful artist and entrepreneur."*

Then we were able to do a little visualization with young Steph where she was able to joyfully be in the zone creating art and there was a line of customers who came to purchase her paintings. The neighbors came over to buy, her babysitter visited to buy, and even Grandpa and Harry ended up swooping up the rest of the remaining inventory. We imprinted this new picture, noticing as many details as possible: the colors, the feelings, and the new empowering belief, *"Everyone loves buying my art and I create it joyfully."*

The biggest takeaway for me about this experience is the fact that I had seen this over and over again in my life: Two people could take the exact same action steps in business and have a dramatically different outcome. Why would that be? If two people have a similar quality product, similar pricing, invest the same amount of money in marketing and labor, spend the same amount of hours launching and promoting, have the same quality website and social media presence, how could one be wildly successful and the other be a total flop?

There is much more to it than dumb luck, and it is more tied to these limiting beliefs that we created, probably a long time ago, that may not even be ours, but beliefs that we adopted along the way. Our beliefs are always there, under the surface, influencing our energy as we make money decisions.

Are you aware of any limiting beliefs around money, business, finance, or prosperity that may be lurking under the surface of your life and wreaking havoc on your success? If you have been blocked in the past or feel that your sensitivity keeps you out of the success club, I have some good news for you. This first step in the process of emotional freedom around money is self-aware-ness. Like most of my tapping programs, I created a twenty-one-day tapping program for working through money stuff (found at stephdodds.emotionalfreedomacademy.com) and below I will show you how to lead yourself through this process.

Step 1: How do you feel about money? For example, anger that others have more than you; sadness because there have been so many money mistakes in your past; frustration because no matter how hard you work, there never seems to be enough money, and so on.

Step 2: Ask yourself what you are sure is true about money? What are some things that you were taught about how money works and how to obtain it? What beliefs about finances may have been passed down to you by parents, teachers, or authority figures?

Step 3: Visualize what success would look like for you? Really think about this. What is standing in your way of this picture of success?

Just like the other topics, this is not the time to think positive, be nice, or fair, or politically correct. Are you starting to see a theme now? It is time to talk about the negative aspects, so that you can name them, be with them, and then tap them out of your system gracefully.

You can use the same tapping for money template that I use in the twenty-one-day tapping for prosperity and abundance course: Week 1: Emotions, Week 2: Beliefs, and Week 3: Tapping into a Prosperity Mindset. Please make this your own so it can work the best for you.

Week 1 / Step 1 from above: **How do you feel about money? What is your experience with money? Write down what comes up with each word/emotion below:**

Money stress:

Financial frustration:

Feelings about debt (whether to have it or not):

Fear and overwhelm:

Sadness and defeat:

Worthiness of financial abundance:

Week 2 / Step 2 from above: **Looking for what beliefs are there. Be mindful of any "this is just the way it is" conclusions.**

I am not good with money:

Life is so expensive:

I can't make money doing what I love:

Getting rich is not for me; it's for other people:

Can't have more money than other people:

Must work hard to make money:

Working through money mistakes and forgiveness:

***Week 3 / Step 3 from above:* What would success look like? How would you move through the world if you did not have any distress about money?**

Money is all around me:

I am designed for success:

My income is constantly increasing:

Trusting the divine and myself:

Booming business success:

I am worthy:

I am grateful in advance for:

After taking some notes on the above emotions and statements, ask yourself if any new insights have arisen. These awarenesses are the golden nuggets we are mining in the subconscious mind. If we are unaware of the "writing on our walls," we will be stuck with the reality of "I can't make money doing what I love" or whatever disempowering belief is there, for our whole lives. Because we use money every day, and it essentially touches most parts of our lives, sometimes continuous tapping is required on this topic.

I will use an example from the Abraham-Hicks book *Money and the Law of Attraction*: If you are in the store grocery shopping and you notice that the organic eggs you usually buy are now three dollars more than they usually are, it can start a thought spiral. "Life is getting so expensive; how am I supposed to afford my favorite foods if the prices keep going up, my living wage is the same, but my living expenses keep rising? I feel like I can never get ahead; this is so discouraging and frustrating, and if only I had bought that house ten years ago I would be in a lot better place right now."

A spiral of thoughts toward the negative can happen in an instant, but now we have tapping that can disrupt that negative thought pattern and get us back on track on a thought pattern that knows we live in an abundant universe and that all is well.

Our attitudes and feelings create our experience, and our inner world creates our outer world. We desire money because we want the feeling and experience we believe the money will give us. This desire is natural and a good thing; it is good to want to feel good. Money is just energy like everything else, and our feelings about it may be the very thing that is keeping it at a distance. All money does is go in circles; it changes hands, and it moves from one person to the next. And if we feel tight about it, money will be tight. The wonderful thing about being sensitive is that you are most likely very intuitive. So once you clean out the energetic blocks to wealth, you will have an advantage because you will be in tune and able to listen deeply to your inner guidance when it comes to decision-making, dream planning, and deciding what is possible for you.

Journaling exercise for tapping on money stuff:

- What feelings come up when I think about giving or receiving money?

- If money were a person or character in my life, would I have a good relationship with them?

- How has money been a blessing in my life? How has it been a challenge in my life?

- How would I like to feel about money? And what is standing in the way of me feeling that?

- If money and I were besties, how would my life look different?

11: Achievements & Goals

"Because you are alive, everything is possible."

—Thich Nhat Hanh

Tapping can help support individuals in getting out of their own way to accomplish goals. Have you ever felt sabotaged by, well, yourself? Or your emotional response? Or found it hard to focus on what you need to do because you are feeling so intensely? Tapping gives you the opportunity to deal with the emotion, cry, and get out whatever you need to, so you can come to a calm and peaceful place again to accomplish achievements.

Sensitive people tend to have a harder time in the corporate world, keeping high-demand job positions, and oftentimes end up being entrepreneurs. This is so they have their own space to create, and they only have one person to manage: themselves. They are more prone to overwhelm and overstimulation, which can easily happen when events outside of our control pile a long list of to-dos onto us. Even if they are lucky enough to be a successful solopreneur, they may still run into difficult customers, intense clients, and straight-up mean online reviews from Internet trolls. I am not saying being an entrepreneur is easy; I'm just saying it might be a better environment for some. Sensitive types tend to feel safe among trusted friends and family but have a hard time compartmentalizing for work and not bringing their sensitivity to the workplace. Because well, it is a part of them that is not celebrated in most workplaces. Many sensitive people get discouraged because they have struggled in jobs with mean bosses or who simply can't tolerate a toxic environment, and are not sure why this whole "career" thing seems to be so easy for everyone else.

The good news is that sensitive people are natural leaders who can be wildly successful, especially with the right support around them. With the right supportive environment, encouragement, and trusted guidance, sensitive people can absolutely flourish. EFT tapping can be a support to those who are not in the most beneficial environment, or who simply get distracted by other people's icky energy, or need help rerouting back into alignment after a tough day of defeat.

Staying in Alignment

I have seen the same chiropractor for the last five years. My neck hurt every day for a long time, and I am grateful to report that now my neck only hurts every once in a while. When my neck hurts I actually think to myself, wow, there was a time when I felt this crappy all of the time. My doctor does a little scan on the back of the neck for each patient who comes into her office, each time they come in. A little graph prints out of a tiny machine and it tells her where you may be out of alignment. Because I have been going to her for so long, she is able to track progress and notice patterns. One Monday morning after a fun weekend of activity, I knew I needed to call Dr. Desiree. My neck hurt pretty bad. Perhaps it was all the twisting from my wonky golf swing this weekend? It didn't matter what happened at this point; I needed some help.

The doctor scanned my neck, saw the graph and noticed a pattern. She told me that I had been doing pretty well lately but my alignment hasn't looked this bad since the previous October. She asked me if there was any kind of significant event that happened in a past October that could be triggering this subluxation. She said that she has had many patients who had lost a family member, got some upsetting news, or had a big life change in the same month, and when their body gets triggered and remembers the trauma each year it pulls them out of alignment again. I thought about it for a moment. Well, I did get laid off from my job on October 1, a couple of years ago. When this happened, I found myself in a big spiral of "what the heck am I doing with my life" type of thinking. You know, instead of relaxing and trusting everything was going to turn out just fine, if not better than before, and know that perhaps this change was an incredible gift.

My mind raced with fear of starting a new profession in a brand-new industry and starting from scratch. I was thirty-five years old at the time (which now I understand is very young), but I was scared that it was too late for me. I had thoughts of being off track, lost, and a whole lot of confusion mixed in with some self-doubt. Looking back on this time, I can see clearly that I was completely capable and wish I would have viewed my circumstances as an exciting fresh start.

I shared this with my chiropractor. She said this made sense because our thoughts can throw us out of alignment all of the time. In fact, it doesn't matter how many times she adjusts someone; if they keep thinking the same misaligned thoughts over and over, they are going to keep throwing themselves out of whack, over and over. Just like misaligned thoughts can throw everything off.

In this chapter, I am going to share how you can use EFT to support issues like procrastination, being frozen in overwhelm, and how to get your thoughts in the right alignment for success and triumphant achievements. The truth is that you can accomplish anything that you set your mind to, especially if you tap away the emotional disruption that creates the same self-sabotage patterns that have held you back in the past. Imagine a life where you are able to tap on your own feelings about the project that flopped, the frustration of the current project you are working on, or the lack of motivation you are experiencing. With EFT, you will have a best friend in your back pocket who can help you through these times so that failure does not stop you anymore.

What we focus on is what grows. Great oak trees start from a single seed. From seed, we need to water, prune, and tend to the budding new life if we want it to grow. If you have big dreams, all sorts of obstacles can pop up to test our strength, commitment, and stick-to-it-ness. All things have a chance of life if we give them our full attention and tender loving care. The key is to get back on track faster instead of rerouting for hours, days, or weeks.

Mae

Mae was an entrepreneur, but she was not in a place yet where she was able to only run her business as her full-time gig. She was looking for something to support her income while she continued to grow her business as a freelance writer. One day she had the idea of becoming a substitute teacher. This way she could substitute Mondays and Fridays, and work on her writing projects midweek. She would not need to sub if she was crushing it that particular month, and she could sub as much as she wanted too if it was a slow time in her business. She had the perfect plan, but there was a big step she needed to take in order to make this plan come to fruition, and that was passing the CBEST test, the California Basic Educational Skills Test. This test typically takes three hours and has three major components to it: reading comprehension, writing, and math.

She was pretty confident when it came to reading and writing, but the math portion scared the you know what out of her. She happened to be married to a fifth-grade teacher, so the math tutoring began shortly after she had scheduled her test date. She studied for the next two months, doing more long division, geometry, and calculating than she had done in the previous twenty years combined. She had lots of teachers in her community, and when Mae shared that she was planning on taking the CBEST and becoming a substitute teacher, they all had a story about the test. One friend said that it took her three times to pass the test, another said that her husband is a lawyer and he failed the test on his first attempt, and another friend said, "Good thing I took that when I was twenty years old because there is no way I could do this now."

Still, Mae had been studying and set on just doing the best that she could.

The morning of the test, her husband gave her a simple multiplying fractions problem, and Mae's mind went blank. She became wide-eyed and tears started to well up. "OMG, I have no idea." Her husband encouraged her, reminding her that she had done this many times before successfully. But she went blank and started to get nervous. Her palms were suddenly sweaty, a headache came on, and she could feel her heart beating in her chest. In this moment she felt a tremendous amount of pressure, like the weight of the world was riding on her ability to pass this test and she was buckling. She phoned a friend to help, one of her tapping buddies who was a skilled practitioner.

"Do you have time for an emergency session today? I am having a legit test-anxiety freak-out," she said.

Luckily her friend was able to squeeze her in that day. Mae was instantly in tears when the session started, and let her friend know that her feelings were incredibly intense.

"Perhaps I am being hijacked by a younger version of myself, because I had this crippling test anxiety as a kid," she added.

They tapped and tapped together:

[Setup statement] *"Even though I am feeling all of this anxiety about this test, and I am panicking because I drew a blank for this math problem today, I still deeply love and completely accept myself."*

[Reminder phrases] *"This anxiety about this test, this fear I feel, all of this pressure I feel, even though I have been studying for two months, I drew a blank today about multiplying fractions, and it really scared me. All of this pressure I feel, this fear of failing, it feels like so much is riding on this. If I don't pass this test, I may have to get a full-time job and give up on my dreams of being a freelance writer. All of this intensity, I had the same test anxiety as a kid, and it feels like so much more is riding on this one test right now. I am connected to my younger self right now, there is an open channel of energy from her to me, and all of her intense feelings are rushing into my body—I am feeling everything that she is feeling. Right now I am going to use this open channel to send her some love, and let her know this is all going to be OK. Even if I do fail this test, it may not impact my life all that much; I may just need to take it again. I am letting my body, mind and spirit know right now that all will be well, no matter what the outcome is."*

After tapping and tapping and crying and crying with her friend, Mae smiled, laughed a bit at herself, and said, "Well, ha ha, I guess it wouldn't really be that big of a deal if I had to take the test again. I do feel so much better; what a relief."

She admitted that she was a little embarrassed that she had such a dramatic reaction, but her friend reminded her that when we get hijacked by our younger selves, it is really difficult for our logical minds to win over the emotional response. Mae thanked her friend, washed her face, and started to get ready for the test. Her test was at 6 p.m., and she had until 10 p.m. to complete it.

When she arrived at the test center, she felt grounded, focused, and was ready to give it her best shot. She also had a healthy amount of nonattachment to the outcome going for her.

She took her time and stayed present with each question. When she hit submit on the last question, tears welled up in her eyes again, but this time it was because she was so proud of herself. This was a success story in her book because of the night and day difference in experiences she would have had if she did not do an hour of tapping with her friend. A week later, Mae got her test results back, and she passed! Not only did she pass each section of the test, but she also actually scored the highest in the math section.

Workplace Relationships

Similar to what we learned in chapter nine about relationships, if you are having a hard time with a coworker or boss, simply make a bullet point list about all of the things that bother you about this person, find the main emotion that you feel, and tap on all of the aspects that are bugging you. This way you will be able to clean up the debris in your energy, and that person is freed up to show up in a whole new way.

Also, tapping aside, setting healthy boundaries at work is just as important as it is anywhere else. Ask for what you need and take the time off that you need. Your peace is worth it and you are likely a huge asset to the company or project. If you are well taken care of, you will be a much better employee and business person; you will be more creative and stronger as the natural problem-solver that you are. And let's face it, some work environments are just too toxic for sensitive beings.

If you decide that a workplace is not right for you, that is OK. If you need to walk away, sometimes that is the absolute best self-care. If you are dealing with people at work who are narcissists or sociopaths it may be the best decision to remove yourself from the situation. Empathic and sensitive people can be targets of narcissists because they want the magic that you have naturally. True narcissists often get jealous, want to make everything your fault, and take pleasure in taking you down. I hate to say it, but if a situation is truly toxic, no amount of growth, self-care or tapping can help. The best option is to shift gears and focus on finding a new job or situation to place your energy. If you are nervous about finding a new job, or have job interview nerves, tap on those nerves. I would encourage you to keep tapping regardless because you do not want to attract the same toxic work environment over and over again. To upgrade your reality, the more tapping the better.

Big Goals

If you have a big dream or goal that feels out of reach, ask yourself, what is standing in the way of me achieving this goal? Journal about the answer that you get. This is your tapping script. We will learn more about this technique in the next chapter with the VOC.

Procrastination

When struggling with procrastination, simply tapping on resistance to doing a certain task can be very helpful. Even if you are lying down in a warm bed, and do not want to get up, you can tap on the level of resistance you feel. For example:

[Setup statement] *"Even though I am feeling all of this resistance to getting out of bed and going to work today, I still deeply love and completely accept myself."*

[Reminder phrases] *"All of this resistance, don't want to go to work today, all of this resistance I feel, I actually love myself for not wanting to go to work today, I have better things to do like resting or playing. Even though I am feeling all of this resistance, and I definitely don't want to go, I really can get out of bed right now. Maybe I can shift my thinking here, maybe today will be a fantastic day, especially if I let go of these grumpy, resistant feelings, maybe I will get a raise today, maybe I will meet the love of my life at work today, maybe I could even make someone else's day today. You never know; weirder things have happened. Even though I have this remaining resistance, I am just going to honor it right now. I love the part of me that wants to stay in bed, and I love the part of me that is committed to getting up and doing a great job at work today. I am going to give myself one more moment to rest, and then when I count down from five, I am going to leap out of bed to start the day. Five, four, three, two, one, blast off!"*

When I was writing this book, I wanted to distract myself from doing the work by eating, drinking, scrolling through social media, and cleaning the house. I was sure there must be a grain of rice somewhere on the floor in the kitchen that I wouldn't want anyone to step on. Everything seemed to want to pull me away from this big goal. I decided to lead a tapping and writing group; this way, I would have the dedicated time, no matter what, because I was leading the group. Being a leader was great accountability because I had to show up every week, no matter what resistance, tasks, or obligations showed up that evening during writing time. We would log on to Zoom, tap for about fifteen minutes, and then shut up and write. The participants reported that they were more focused on their writing process, their flow of words became more effortless, and the process was more productive after the tapping. It was a win-win. Tapping can support productivity of all kinds. Be sure to check out my YouTube channel for the productivity playlist, which has tapping for an overwhelming amount of to-do lists, technical difficulty frustrations, job interview nerves, and of course, creative writing! Tapping can support productivity of all kinds.

Journaling exercise for tapping on achievements and goals:

- Am I in an environment where I can flourish professionally?

- What is standing in the way of my success?

- Do my goals feel achievable? If not, why?

- If I had all the money I needed, would I still be doing what I am currently doing professionally?

- How have I persevered in the past? What can I be proud of myself for today?

12: Creativity, Flow, and Going for Your Dreams

"Creativity is intelligence having fun."

—Albert Einstein

I love it when people tell me that they are not creative. Who me? I could never dabble in watercolors, take a pottery class, or write a romantic poem. This is how most people think of creativity as the expression of an art form. I would like you to start thinking about creativity in a new way, as no matter how creative you believe that you are, you are constantly creating, all of the time. You create in every moment with your thoughts, beliefs, actions, and attitudes. Your thoughts, emotions, and perspectives are created right now as you read this. You are taking my words in through your perceptual filter and assessing whether they are true or not, relating to them, and creating your own spin on them.

A sensitive person is connected to the divine. True empaths know what others are feeling without that other person saying something. You may pick up on things that other people don't. You may know things, and you are unsure how you know them. If you are sensitive and stressed or overstimulated, it can wreak havoc on your creative process. Precious creative energy ends up being utilized to put up a defensive, protective shield so that you can regain yourself again.

You are literally creative potential walking around. You are a channel whether you like it or not. Think about a fresh tomato being plucked from the vine for dinner tonight. Imagine the deep red color and juiciness filled with nutritious life force energy. Now imagine a tomato that was picked weeks ago to ripen on a truck as it travels across the country. It was probably picked green, and because it has been disconnected from the vine for some time, it has less nutrition to offer by the time it makes it to the dinner table. Tapping can keep things fresh and give you an abundance of juicy ideas available to you at any time.

Suppose your emotional freedom garden is not tended to, your life force can be cut off from the following activities: writing, making music, cooking and recipe creation, photography, dancing, teaching, running a business, speaking, sewing, homemaking, raising children, problem-solving, making essential oil blends or healing salves, sexuality, making jewelry, or leading a ceremony.

Everyday stress and overwhelm can take away from creative activities because our energy is being used for other things. I had a boyfriend once I would watch come home from a long workday and have just enough energy to make dinner and be in bed by 9 p.m. But after he'd had two weeks of vacation, he was writing funny songs while playing his slide guitar and making new dinner creations for fun.

As I mentioned in the previous chapter, I used EFT many times to support the process of writing this book. I sat down and tapped for almost every writing session. During the times when I would be staring at a blank page and wasn't sure what to write about, I would remember, "Oh yeah, I haven't tapped yet. No wonder I am feeling stuck." I was able to tap away the everyday distractions of life and any resistance or doubt I was feeling that day to get in the zone and start typing away. This book was already in me, and I just needed to tap on the aspects that were standing in the way of getting it out of me and onto the page.

Consider that your creativity benefits not only you, but many others, creating a ripple effect of joy. You see, your creations may inspire other people, maybe the song that healed someone's heart, the book that changed someone's life, or the painting that brought someone to tears of awe. A dear friend of mine inspires me daily the way she is creative in parenting, caring for the planet by not using plastic products, and being a beekeeper. Consider that we are all divine channels for goodness to come through us, and our sensitivity acts like an antenna, and we are able to be deep listeners.

Do you ever feel like you have a creative project in you, and you are not sure how to materialize it? You can tap on what you believe is standing in the way of your creative flow, perhaps not having enough time, the right materials, or even thinking you need to have more skill. All of the creative energy that you dream of is already available, and it has been available the whole time. You will find supportive tap-a-long videos on my YouTube playlist, "Tapping for Creativity," with topics such as Unleashing Creativity, Tapping for Writer's Block, Fear of Being Seen, and Tapping for Doing Creative Work with Joy.

In Pam Grout's book *E2*, I love the story she shares about the aha moment she had about the ever-abundant universe while visiting Esalen on the California coast. She and her friend arrived later in the evening for their visit, and it was a bit dark and cold in the room they were staying in. They shivered and cuddled close for warmth during the night. In the morning, they awoke to find a plug-in wall heater right next to them. This heater was there the entire time to support them, and so is this ever-loving universe, even if we cannot see it at the moment. This is how I imagine creative potential, it is right there waiting for us, and all we need to do is literally plug into it to access it and ride the wave of creativity and flow.

Breaking through Resistance

One of my tapping colleagues and friends, Brad Yates, and I were doing an online Zoom interview one day prior to the launching of this book. He asked me at what level I would say

I felt resistance to putting my book out there? I thought about it for a moment. I was extremely comfortable sharing my work with my five writing besties, but sharing it with the world, yikes! I was surprised that I had a level 7 resistance, and I wasn't exactly sure why. He led me through a few rounds of tapping, and by the end, I was ready to holler from the rooftops that my book was available to purchase. I felt peace in knowing that my book wasn't for everyone, but for those whom it would benefit, it would be a great gift.

He then shared a story with me about his own creativity breakthrough. Brad had written a children's book about tapping, *The Wizard's Wish*. He has also been an artist and cartoonist most of his life and was planning on doing his own illustrations for the book. He wrote the text for the book, and then it sat there for two years without illustrations. He then reached out to a tapping friend and had a private EFT session with her. Within the next week after the session, Brad had created forty illustrations for his book, and now it is available to the world.

Going for Your Dreams

Creativity expands beyond our day-to-day lives and makes up our lives as a whole. When you dream about what is possible for your life, that is creative energy.

What would it look like if you could be fearlessly *YOU* and show up in your life feeling confident and comfortable with yourself in every major area? The thing is, there is only one YOU. No one has your exact perspective, stories, voice, skill set, sensitivity superpowers, and unique take on life. If you use the road map I'm about to introduce, you will truly be able to upgrade your life from the inside out and shine as your most authentic you.

I want you to think about seven areas of your life right now that can use an upgrade. I am going to guide you on how I have done this process for myself and have guided my clients through these steps, but I ask you to please make this experience your own. I want you to feel free to edit/change/adjust this to work for you. The road map on the next page is inspired by a combination of the Wheel of Life used by Tony Robbins and others, and the chakra energy system to create these areas, as I find that they cover all of the bases naturally.

Sacred Seven Areas of Life:

1. Self-Preservation: Money/finances/knowing my place in the world

2. Self-Gratification: Creativity/trust/flow/sensuality

3. Self-Confidence: Personal power & physical health

4. Self-Love: Relationships, including romantic, friends, family, professional

5. Self-Expression: Speaking truth, voice, interaction, fun, and recreation

6. Self-Reflection: Vision & personal growth

7. Self-Knowledge: Spirituality & connection to a higher power

Visual of Seven Sacred areas of Life / Chakra Energy Centers:

7th Chakra, Crown Chakra
Crown of the head
Purple - Thought Element

6th Chakra, Third Eye Chakra
Above Brow Line
Deep Indigo - Light Element

5th Chakra, Throat Chakra
Base of Neck
Bright Blue - Sound Element

4th Chakra, Heart Chakra
Behind the heart
Green – Air Element

3rd Chakra, Solar Plexus
At base of Rib Cage
Yellow – Fire Element

2nd Chakra, Sacral Chakra
Just below the navel
Orange – Water Element

1st Chakra, Root Chakra
Base of Spine
Red – Earth Element

Life Upgrade Exercise

This exercise is a way to organize your thoughts and get clear on the areas of your life you would like to transform for the better. Know that it is OK to have many drafts and create this as a working document.

Step 1: Create an affirmation for the top of Worksheet #1 (end of chapter). What are three words you can use to describe your best self? For word ideas, see Worksheet #2 (at the end of this chapter).

Step 2: Find a picture of yourself that you absolutely LOVE, to place in the center heart of Worksheet #1. You can attach it with tape or a glue stick—get creative with this. This picture will represent your most *you-est*, you, in all of your glory, living your best life.

Step 3: Gaze at your Worksheet #1 and remember these seven areas of life that you would like to upgrade.

Step 4: Think about what belief you have about yourself or about life in each given area that may be holding you back. (Yes, we are still focusing on the negative for now.) On Worksheet #1, write the belief on the line with the corresponding number.

Step 5: Pick a belief you would like to start with, or you can simply go in order, starting with number one (self-preservation) and work through these beliefs. You may do this work on your own, but I highly recommend signing up to work through this with a practitioner. Bring this list with you and let your practitioner know that you want to upgrade these areas of your life. If they are certified in both EFT and Matrix Reimprinting / Hacking Reality, they will be able to help you and guide you to find exactly when this disempowering belief was created, and tap with that younger self who created it in an effort to make sense of life. Once tapping is complete, you will be able to create a new empowering brief to take its place. Once you do that, replace each and every line with the new empowering belief. I like to write on a separate piece of paper and using a glue stick, paste my new awesome, supportive belief on top of the old one. If you commit to this process, you have a beautiful piece of art full of your new empowering beliefs. This can be something to refer back to as you continue to reinforce and solidify your life upgrade in each area.

Personal Peace Procedure

Another way to completely uplevel your life is to follow Gary Craig's Personal Peace Procedure. This is where you write down a list of many challenging or traumatic memories from the past, organize them into categories, and give each one a simple title. For example, when I was little, I loved the tiny snails in our garden. I was probably four years old, so I did not know at the time that snails were garden pests. My cousin saw my excitement while gazing at the snails and informed me that snails love to eat salt. As you can imagine this story ended up being a traumatic memory in my Personal Peace Procedure. I gave it a title—*cousin snail memory*—and tapped on the emotional components that came up around the memory. If you would like to do the Personal Peace Procedure, I recommend doing it at a time in your life when you are in a really good place and have the space to drum up old memories to work through. It may not be supportive if you are going through a breakup, a health crisis, or a big transition. However, if you are able to work through a long list of memories, imagine the amount of emotional freedom you will experience. This process has the potential to completely upgrade your life from the inside out, the ultimate emotional freedom garden makeover.

<u>Journaling exercise for tapping to nourish creativity:</u>

- How do I experience creativity?

- What creative activity feels like play to me? When do I feel like I am in the zone?

- What do I know how to do that no one ever taught me how to do? I just started doing it?

- What information do my spirit guides and angels have for me that will be supportive to my creative path?

- What is standing in the way of completely actualizing my dreams?

Worksheet #1

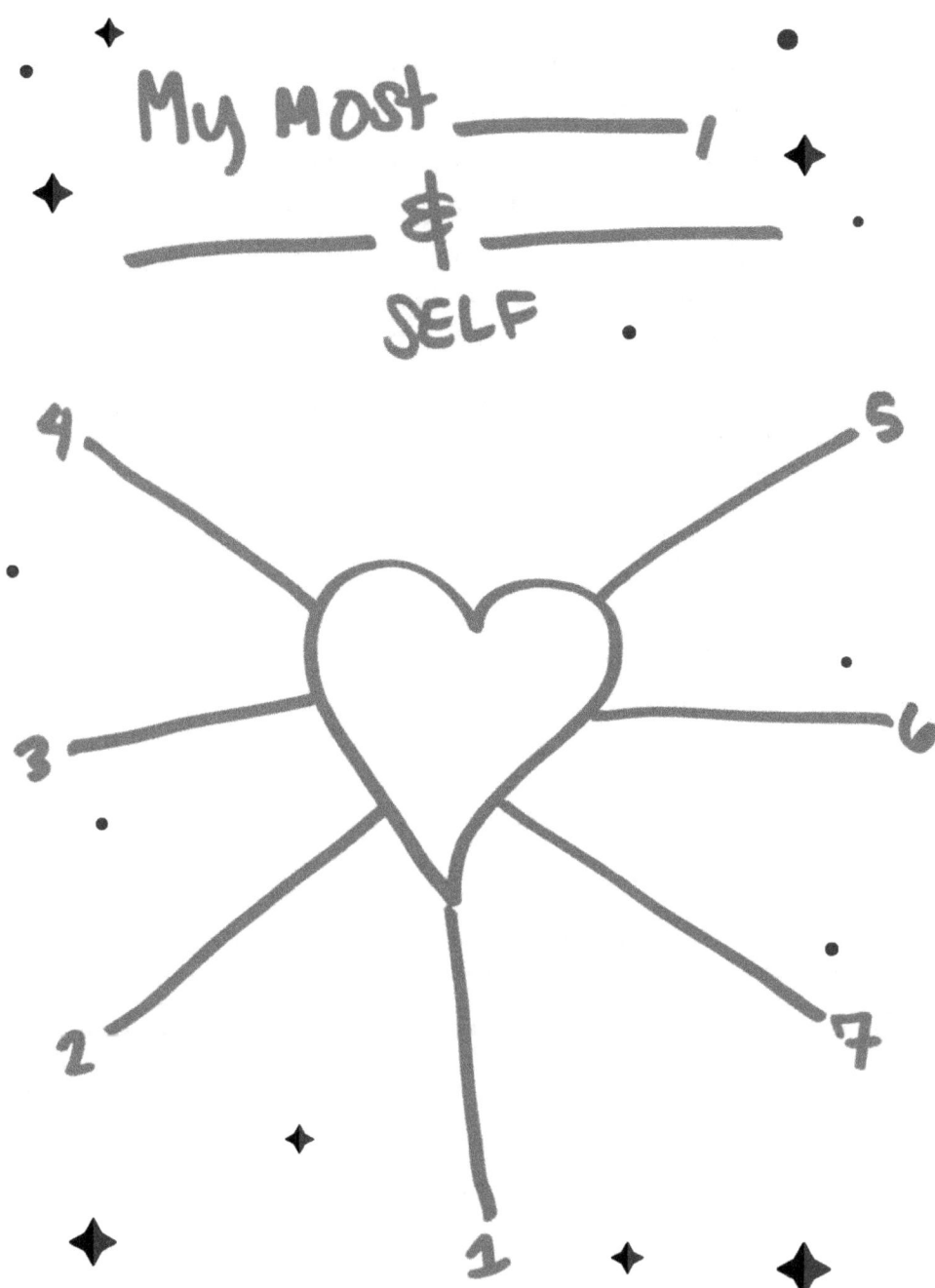

My most _____ 1
_____ & _____
SELF

Worksheet #2

I AM

Abundant Adventurous Affectionate Amazing Ambitious
Amiable Artistic Assertive Athletic Attentive Awesome
Balanced Beautiful Brave Bright Brilliant Buff Calm
Capable Charming Cheerful Chic Clever Competent
Composed Confident Conscientious Considerate
Consistent Content Community Cool Cooperative
Courageous Creative Crafty Curious Decisive Deep
Delightful Devoted Diligent Discerning Eager Easy-going
Efficient Endearing Energetic Enterprising Enthusiastic
Fabulous Family Friendly Freedom Funny Fun Focused
Generous Gentle Graceful Grateful Happy Healthy
Helpful Honest Humorous Imaginative Independent
Inspiring Intelligent Interesting Intuitive Inventive Joyous
Kind Lively Logical Lovable Mature Motivated Musical
Natural Orderly Outgoing Optimistic Passionate Patient
Peaceful Playful Pleasant Polite Positive Powerful
Practical Pretty Prosperous Realistic Reassuring Reliable
Resourceful Respected Responsible Revered Romantic
Sassy Sensible Sensitive Serene Sharp Silly Sincere Smart
Snazzy Sober Sophisticated Soulful Spirited Stable
Steady Strong Sweet Talented Thoughtful Tranquil
Trustworthy Unique Vulnerable Warm Wealthy Willing
Wonderful

THE HARVEST

13: Self-Guided Tapping & Working with Limiting Beliefs

"Remember, you have been criticizing yourself for years and it hasn't worked. Try approving of yourself and see what happens."

—Louise Hay

Now that you know the magic of tapping, I want to share with you the many ways to incorporate tapping into your life on a very practical and doable level. The absolute best way to get started with EFT is to work with an experienced practitioner you are drawn to, whom you get results with, and whom you resonate with. This allows you to have some guidance, and this person can be a mirror for you, offering ideas and higher perspectives you may not have thought of. For some, this may be more relaxing as you will not need to be so self-aware and you can be lovingly guided by another. If that is not available to you currently, there are ways to start tapping for yourself right away for issues you would like to work on as well as limiting beliefs.

Tapping for Yourself on YouTube

Tapping along with YouTube videos can be a quick and affordable way to get started. This is how I started tapping myself, as a daily practice, following along with my tiny phone screen in the living room. I had a lovely private yoga client at the time, Penny. She would come over to my place, and we would do yoga for thirty-five minutes, tap for five to ten minutes depending on how long the video was that day, and then sit in meditation together for another five minutes. When we were done with the little video, we would look at each other, smile, and say, "Love that Brad Yates." I tapped along with Brad Yates on YouTube for two years before I ever decided to dive in and learn more for myself.

There are many topics available on YouTube from test-taking nerves, to releasing guilt when holding healthy boundaries, and even lowering tension contributing to teeth grinding. As we know, EFT works the best the more specific we get. The downside to tapping on YouTube is that in order for it to be helpful, you must find a video that really speaks to exactly what you're going through in that moment. Simply type into a search on YouTube what you're looking for (stress, overwhelm, getting a good night's sleep, and so on) and there should be plenty of videos available to use. Give it a try . . . Even if the video is just *close enough* to what you would like to feel relief about. Feel free to use your own words when tapping along with the video to make it more specific for you. Snoop around and search for EFT tappers to follow. My top favorites are Brad Yates and Margaret Lynch, and of course, I think my channel is pretty groovy too.

Tapping with Yourself in the Mirror

One of the benefits of tapping by yourself is that you can really *let it rip*. Even more potently, using a mirror while tapping can help you reach deep soul wisdom. You can say whatever you need to say. You can just tap, rant, and literally say all of the things you might otherwise hold in because you don't want to hurt someone's feelings and are *not supposed to feel what you really feel*. Following the basic recipe from chapter 3, or my protocol from chapter 8, all you need is a notebook and a mirror, and it is completely possible to lead yourself. Not sure what to say? Get started by journaling, writing everything out, and brain dump it all onto some paper or in your EFT notebook. There may be many emotions on your paper, but see if you can narrow it down to one. If you can spot the main emotion, use that to create a setup statement and then tap, tap, tap through the reminder phrases. Speak your truth as you look into your own eyes in the mirror and hold a sacred space for yourself. Notice as you go that you may feel a shift or see signs of energy shifting in your reflection. It is also possible to do this on your phone mirror or in a Zoom meeting just with yourself.

Affirmation-Based Tapping

Affirmation-based tapping is not only one of the most enjoyable versions of tapping, but it is also a vehicle for the most profound change-work for letting go of limiting beliefs available today. It all starts with what Gary Craig calls the *Writing on Our Walls*. Our limiting beliefs are not visible to us, but they are oh-so-powerful and potentially dangerous blind spots. Limiting beliefs are our environment, our surroundings; they are the writing on our walls. They are the lens through which we view the world. This is a good thing if we have rose-colored lenses and have beliefs like *"Success is inevitable for me"* or *"I am lovable and capable."* They become a problem if we don't have rose-colored lenses but have shit-goggles. Examples of shit-goggle beliefs would be *"Nice guys finish last"* and *"I can't make money doing what I love."* When someone challenges an ingrained belief, it is as if they are telling you the sky isn't blue, or that dairy is not the reason you get so bloated after a meal. What the heck do they know? They are trying to tell you your reality isn't your reality, which usually doesn't go over well.

The writing on our walls is helpful in many ways. For example, if you drive up to a stoplight and it is red, yellow or green, the writing on your walls informs you of what to do. If you are out for a nice dinner and the waiter brings you some soup, the writing on your walls informs you whether you eat the soup with your knife, fork, or spoon. Rob Nelson refers to this as our operating system in his book *Hacking Reality*. To us, the writing on our walls is just "how life is" but to others, it may sound a little cray cray. As EFT practitioners, when we hear writing on the walls, we say yay! Because we know what we are working with and we can chisel away at any beliefs we are holding that are not supporting the best version of ourselves.

This nifty system we will be using below is called the VOC, Validity of Cognition. The VOC is a self-assessment, a measurement of a belief and its trueness. You get to inquire about what feels real on certain statements, including affirmations. This is not a judgment thing; it is a self-assessment thing. Half of you will just have a number pop into your head right away, similar to the SUD level, naturally. The other half will think this is weird and have a hard time getting to a number, but do your best and don't overthink this process. This is a fluid experience and may change from day-to-day.

These affirmations are divided into four categories below: Prosperity & Abundance; Healthy, Happy Body; Self-Love & Relationships; and Creativity, Trust, & Flow. Follow along with me and simply give yourself a rating for each statement from 0 percent true to 100 percent true.

How true are the following statements on a scale of 0–100 percent of *trueness* for you today?

Prosperity, Abundance & Success Affirmations

_____ Money comes to me easily and effortlessly

_____ I am in the flow of abundance

_____ I prosper wherever I turn

_____ I can afford to take time off whenever I need

_____ I am a money magnet

_____ I am peaceful as I manage my finances

_____ I receive money graciously

_____ I am generous

_____ Money is all around me

_____ I have a great relationship with money

_____ I am a good steward of money. I spend some and save some

_____ I spend my money on products and experiences I am aligned with

_____ My income is constantly increasing

_____ I am worthy of prosperity

_____ I am designed for success

_____ I am an intelligent business person

_____ My financial future looks bright

_____ My financial dreams are within reach

_____ Living debt-free is for me

_____ I am clear and confident with my money decisions

Healthy, Happy Body Affirmations

_____ I honor my body's divine intelligence

_____ My body and I are on the same team

_____ My body heals itself efficiently and automatically

_____ I take fantastic care of myself

_____ I am filled with life force and energy

_____ I maintain my ideal healthy weight easily

_____ I am strong and capable

_____ I see my body with the eyes of love

_____ I am flexible and move with ease

_____ I love living pain-free

_____ I digest and assimilate all of life's experiences

_____ I get healthier every year

_____ I take full responsibility for my own well-being

_____ I crave healthful foods

_____ I move my body with joy

_____ I take steps every day to improve my well-being

_____ I am patient and kind with my body

_____ I am worthy of health and happiness

_____ It is safe for me to stay connected to my body

_____ My body deserves the best

_____ I am kind to my body as it ages and as it changes

_____ I am my own authority. I make decisions for my body's highest good

Self-Love & Romance Affirmations

_____ It is safe for me to love and be loved

_____ I am loved for who I really am

_____ What I want wants me

_____ My needs are important and valid

_____ I am taken care of now and always

_____ I take good care of my relationships

_____ I am emotionally available

_____ I create and honor healthy boundaries that serve myself and others

_____ I am good-looking

_____ Someone thinks of me during the day and smiles

_____ I am a good communicator

_____ My heart is full

_____ I am attractive and attracting love

_____ I am seen; I am heard

_____ I can relax and enjoy my relationship

_____ I can trust myself and trust my partner

_____ I am whole and complete no matter what my relationship status is

_____ I am open to deep connection

_____ I am perfectly imperfect

_____ My partner loves me

_____ I am adored for all my quirks

_____ I love me

_____ I relax and recognize my self-worth

_____ I am good enough

Creativity, Trust & Flow

_____ The Universe has my back

_____ I am a writer. My words flow easily and effortlessly

_____ I am a creative genius

_____ I am an artist

_____ I surrender to my general awesomeness

_____ I am constantly generating brilliant ideas

_____ I am creating a life I love

_____ I trust myself and my path

_____ I joyfully learn from my life experiences

_____ It is safe for me to live my life fully and freely

_____ It is safe for me to let go of the past; I am free now

_____ I make time and space for my creative expression

_____ I am full of creative energy

_____ My art is highly valued and appreciated

_____ I surrender to the flow of life; I trust the process

_____ I have natural talent

_____ I trust my intuition and divine guidance

_____ I am smart

_____ Innovative ideas and creative solutions come naturally
to me

_____ I allow myself to daydream and use my imagination

_____ I am a visionary

_____ I am an unlimited creative creature

How did you do? Take a moment to look over your answers. Were you surprised by anything? Take a moment to journal about your self-assessment exercise if any insights come through.

There is a reason why affirmations don't work for most of us, most of the time. What we are really affirming, after we declare a powerful statement, is the tailender of the affirmation. What comes *after* that statement is what we're really creating. Most law of attraction information out there does not take into consideration what the subconscious mind's agenda is. Logically we want this affirmation to come true.

One morning, one of the participants in my tapping group revealed that she had noticed a pattern while doing the assessment above. She noticed that the money section was dramatically worse than the other sections. A childhood memory came up for her where she was given little golden toy-money tokens as a gift, but the gift actually stressed her out. Instead of enjoying and playing with the small coins, she felt a tremendous responsibility with them in her possession. She wanted to hoard them, maybe give them to someone else more responsible, and she was afraid she wouldn't have enough if she lost them. This seemingly innocent gift turned into a source of stress and pressure, and a whole lot of beliefs were affirmed at that time. Even as an adult, she dreaded dealing with finances, and never enjoyed having money. She felt that money was bad or dirty somehow but desperately wanted to have more of it as she had just turned fifty years old and had been barely scraping by most of her life.

A note about this—if memories pop up while tapping, this is a good thing. We actually want to know when the limiting belief or stress was created, so we can go into that memory and help out our younger selves who experienced it. Make note of memories that come up in your EFT journal and bring them to your work with a practitioner or put them on your Personal Peace Procedure list from chapter 12.

If we say an affirmation like *"I have a great relationship with money"* or *"I am a money magnet,"* what we are really affirming is that internal voice piping up after, the big *BUT* on the end of that statement. You may think to yourself, *"I am a money magnet!"* *BUT* . . . I only have one hundred dollars in the bank right now, *BUT* I can't really make money doing what I love. And so on and so forth. The good news is, whatever comes after this big *BUT* becomes our tapping script, and we can turn down the volume knob on it.

This idea is similar to the work of Noah St John's *Afformations*, which you can learn more about at noahstjohn.com. No, that is not a typo. *Afformations* are a different way of presenting affirmations as they are presented in the form of a question. Oftentimes I give *afformation* homework to my clients as a simple, quick, tapping magic trick to use on their own. It can also be a fun exercise for those who do not enjoy focusing on the negative, as we are asking the subconscious a positive question. For example, I will ask my client to tap on their chest and ask out loud to themselves a positive question like the following:

- *Why is it so easy for me to speak confidently in public?*

- *Why is it so easy for me to fall asleep peacefully when I lay down?*

- *Why is it so easy for me to accept love and compliments from others?*

When presented this way, the subconscious mind is now focusing on the positive, or a solution, instead of looking for the problem to fix. I experience this when I hear my inner voice say, *"Yeah, why is it so easy for me to speak confidently in public?"*

I would encourage you to pick an affirmation from above list that resonates with you, or create your own. Choose one that would be the biggest game changer for you if it was 100 percent real and true for you. Open a notebook and draw a big line down the middle. On one side write your affirmation; on the other side write your big *BUTS*, aka the tailenders that pop up (see example table below). Then tap, tap, tap with this new personalized script that you have created.

MY AFFIRMATION	TAILENDERS
I AM A POWERFUL MONEY MAGNET!	

This diagram is the framework for the ultimate self-guided tapping experience. You can use this template to tap on any topic, big or small. Declare your affirmation, and then check in with yourself, asking, "*How true is this statement for me?*" The follow-up question is, "*Why is it not 100 percent true today?*" This gives you the power to make your own tapping scripts over and over again. I recommend doing this exercise in your tapping journal, and the date when you did the work, so you can look back on your progress for each topic.

Troubleshooting

You know how magical tapping is at this point on the journey, but what if tapping seems to not be working? *(Insert gasp sound!)* Yes, believe it or not, sometimes tapping will seem to not be helping the issue that you are working on and there are some steps to take in order to reboot the process while tapping on your own.

If tapping doesn't seem to be working, try the following:

1. Drink some water: I am not sure how the tapping community figured this one out, but water really helps. My guess is that this works because everything in the body works better when we are well hydrated. Every time I sit down with a client for a session, I ask them to bring their water bottle.

2. Get more specific: The biggest culprit of ineffective tapping is not being specific enough. The more specific the better with tapping, always. If you do a round of tapping on yourself and your SUD level number does not drop, ask yourself: *How do I know this is a problem?* See if you can go deeper on the next round.

3. Be persistent: Remember that we are working in the realm of Energy Psychology, while tapping on

the physical body. The physical body is dense, so sometimes there may not be a change right away. Be persistent; there may be some relief if you stay with it and keep tapping a little longer.

4. Check and see if the aspect or emotion has shifted: If you started tapping on anger, and you still feel upset after ten minutes of tapping, ask yourself if you have shifted aspects. Is it still anger that you feel? Or have you shifted to a different emotion without realizing it such as sadness, frustration, or fear?

5. Check for secondary gain: This may be difficult if you are tapping by yourself, as secondary gain usually lives in our blind spots. But some good questions to ask yourself are:

- *Is there an upside to this problem?*

- *Is this problem a solution to a deeper problem?*

For a refresher, we talk about secondary gain in chapter 7 when we talk about addiction.

In summary, I encourage you to start tapping for yourself and to try some of the methods mentioned in this chapter. It is absolutely possible to use tapping as a self-guided wellness practice and a self-care tool. It is absolutely possible for you to believe your "I AM" declaration with more fortitude and gumption. Imagine what would be possible for you without that *BUT* narrative in your subconscious blocking you? The sky is the limit without those limiting beliefs. Of course, I will always say working with an experienced practitioner is the best. However, even if you are working with someone I would encourage you to tap on your own as a daily practice or any time you feel stuck. I always encourage my clients to tap on their own, and then bring the big topics to me that they need additional help with. Stress relief is at the tips of your fingers now, and always!

14: Tapping with Kids, Pets, and Groups

*"Sometimes, the smallest things take up
the most room in your heart."*

—Winnie-the-Pooh

Tapping with Kids

Yes, you can absolutely tap with kids! In fact, tapping is often fun for children and works for them more efficiently than it does for adults. They do not have years of conditioning and practice stuffing their emotions down to keep them together in public as adults do. Kids are fluid. Children can be crying one minute and laughing the next. Kids are in the moment with their emotions; they can be nervous one moment and calm the next. Kids tend to love EFT as well. If you are around a kid and they are upset, scared, or nervous about taking a math test at school, try some tapping with them. You will notice in the scripts below we use slightly different setup language than we do with adults. Language for children should be more age-specific. With words tailored to their understanding, they will most likely start smiling, scamper away, and forget what they were upset about in the first place.

Early in my EFT days, I taught small workshops at my local yoga studio. Somehow, for one of my workshops, the *mom phone tree* was alerted that this workshop was appropriate for children. I looked at the class roster, and there were eight kids signed up to attend the workshop. I gave myself a quick pep talk, *"No F-bombs today, Steph, you can do this."*

I love kids, but I was a bit nervous at first as I was thirty-eight years old, had a dog, and hadn't spent time around many kids in years. It ended up being one of the best workshops I ever taught because when I asked for a volunteer to come tap with me at the front of the room, all of the kids' hands shot up. One eighth-grader came up to tap with me and shared how she was afraid to walk down the hallway at school to get to her locker. We measured the SUD level; her fear was an 8 out of 10. I asked her, why is your fear an 8? She explained that she didn't know from day-to-day, which version of her friends would show up that day. Some days her friends were super friendly. Some days her friends would make rude remarks, which was very confusing, and some days they would not say hi at all. She would question if there was some kind of rumor floating around about her, and the fact that this was unpredictable made her fearful of walking down the hall because she was unsure what version of her friends she would encounter.

We tapped and tapped on fear as the parents' eyes in the audience were wide in anticipation. *"Even though I have no idea what I might expect as I walk down the hallway to my locker, I choose to know that IF my so-called friends are moody that day or rude, it has nothing to do with who I am. I am an amazing kid, and I can feel good about that."* We tapped together in front of the class and eventually got her fear level down to 1 out of 10. Let's manage expectations here; getting to a 0 in middle school may not be possible.

If you have children in your life, I would encourage you to introduce tapping to them as a stress relief technique. Kids can use tapping for all things school-related, including test-taking nerves, performance anxiety in sports, and overcoming self-doubt.

Here are some tips and examples of approaches for tapping with kids:

- Stick to the facts more than focusing on the emotions: Instead of deep diving into their emotional experience, bring a light approach. Facts may sound like this: I have a soccer game today, I had pizza for lunch, there is a monster in my closet, and so on. With adults, we would ask, how does that make you feel? With kids, we can just say, *"Even though I do not know how to do this math problem, I am still a really great kid."* Suppose kids add in the emotional component themself, wonderful. But if not, just sticking to the facts can be really helpful.

- Some kids may be able to use the 0 to 10 scale about how they feel. If that does not come naturally to them, have them show you using their hands as a scale. Hands close together in prayer means they feel good, like the equivalent of a 0. Hands are far apart, meaning they do not feel good. Using this visual reference may be easier for kids to gauge than using numbers; it may even work better for some adults.

- Use their words, even if they don't make sense. For example, if the child is telling you they are upset about the blue frog and the pink elephant, that is all of the information you need to start tapping. *"Even though the blue frog is mean, and now the pink elephant can't drink tea, I am still a really good kid."* This may not make sense to you, but it makes sense to them. That is all that matters!

- The younger the kid is that you are communicating with, simple language works best. For little ones, knowing that their parents are OK and safe is extremely important. Mom leaving the room can feel like a life-or-death situation. A very simple, *"Even though it was a hard day, my mommy is OK and she loves me a whole lot,"* can work extremely well to bring calm to the little one.

- Another way to make tapping fun for kids is using a teddy bear or stuffed animal to demonstrate the tapping points. You can put little stickers on the teddy bear's tapping points and have the little one tap on the bear and then tap on themselves in the same places the bear has stickers. This is a playful way to introduce tapping to children.

- If a child seems sad, and doesn't have the words to communicate, invite them to draw a picture of how they are feeling. If the child draws a picture of a figure sitting alone on the grass with a dark cloud over his head, simply tap on what is drawn in the picture. For example, *"Even though I am sitting alone on the grass, and there is a dark cloud over my head, I am still a wonderful kid."* And as you tap through the points and say the reminder phrases, they can be as simple as *"Just sitting alone, on the grass by myself, and there is a big cloud over my head, this dark cloud, this rain cloud following me around, I am not sure why it is here, but I would like to feel better, and I love that about myself."*

- Some older kids may roll their eyes at first, and think the tapping is kinda dumb, but just do your best to guide them. You can even play with this aspect a little bit . . . tap, tap, tap, *"Even though this tapping is dumb, and it is really not going to help me, I am still open to possibilities, and I love myself for that."* This technique can absolutely be helpful for adults as well who are feeling resistance to the tapping process.

- Teenagers and young adults tend to be more open to tapping videos on YouTube like we talked about in the last chapter. They are already connected to their phones most likely and I find they are more open to the technique if no one is watching them. It can't hurt to send a video or two to them as a trial run.

Surrogate Tapping / Tapping for Pets

Surrogate tapping is essentially a highly concentrated form of prayer. It does not matter if a person/animal is on the other side of the planet or in the apartment next door. You can use surrogate tapping by tuning into that being's energy field. With traditional EFT surrogate work, one would try and embody the person's energy that they would like to work on, and tap on themselves as if they are them. If you are working with a practitioner or have Matrix Reimprinting / Hacking Reality in your toolbox, there are a couple of slightly different, alternative approaches to surrogate work. I prefer to imagine a picture of them, see them in my mind's eye, and essentially feel into their energy and witness a hologram of them. Using this method you can ask this hologram of them, how are they feeling at this moment? And if you're lucky enough to get an answer this gives you some fuel for the tapping process. With pets, we may be able to intuitively know what they're feeling, especially if we are really close with the animal. If you are curious to hear more about this topic, check out Gary Craig's YouTube channel, Gary Craig's *New Think*, to find more inspiring surrogate tapping stories.

Faye

I could tell something was distracting my client when the Zoom window opened and I saw her.

"I was excited for my session today, but I apologize that all I can think about is my little dog, Zeus. He has not been feeling well the last twenty-four hours and I really do not want to take him to the vet. He is having some stomach issues and seems really uncomfortable. The last time I took a dog to the vet, it did not go well and I cannot bear the thought of losing him right now," Faye shared.

I let her know it was no problem, and asked her if she would like to do a little tapping for her doggie, Zeus.

"OMG, you can do that?! Yes, please, I guess it is worth a try. Do I need to go get him and put him on my lap for this?"

"Not really," I said.

I asked her to take a few moments to tune into Zeus's energy to see what was going on with him. I coached her to imagine as if she were him and she could feel what he feels. Faye closed her eyes and did just that. Her eyes popped open, and she said, "Whoa, he feels anxiety." I asked her to imagine her dog in front of her. I let her know that she could tap on this mind's eye image (what I call a hologram) of Zeus's little body as we spoke out the phrases.

"Just imagine him in your mind's eye, out in front of you. You will tap all the way down his body, from his head, down to his tail, and back again," I instructed.

A couple of notes about this: I did not assume that Faye had intuitive powers before we started. I have tried surrogate tapping with hundreds of clients at this point, and it always seems to work. When surrogate tapping for people, you tap on their regular points in your mind's eye. When tapping for pets, I believe it has always been instructed that the human still taps on their regular human tapping points while thinking about the pet. But a few years ago, I took my dog to a holistic veterinarian who did acupuncture on animals. She was helping my pup with some heart issues and placed acupuncture needles on my doggie's head and down her spine to her tail. From that point on, when I did tapping for my dog, I would imagine these same points that I saw in the vet's office. I mention this because I can't cite where this method came from; to the best of my knowledge, it was created in that holistic vet's office that day.

OK, back to Faye and Zeus. As Faye tapped on the hologram of Zeus, I led her based on the information she had given me so far. *"Even though I'm feeling some anxiety, I still am a really great dog. Even though I'm feeling this nervous feeling, this unsettled feeling, the world is actually going through a lot of anxiety right now. Even though I'm just a dog, I'm feeling all that energy that the humans are feeling. Because I can't talk, I'm actually more plugged in to all of the human's crazy energy. I've actually been worried about my mom; I don't like to see her stressed all of the time. It makes my tummy hurt too. Even though I have been carrying this stress around, I am allowed to just be a dog, and I do not need to carry any human stress anymore, as best as I can."*

Weeks later, Faye and I had a follow-up appointment, and she let me know that dear Zeus was doing great. The following day after the session, he ran around the house like his old self again.

A few more points about surrogate tapping:

- In my opinion, it is best to ask permission first when doing some surrogate energy work on a person or an animal. This is a controversial topic that I personally think is pretty fun to discuss with energy workers and healers and hear their opinions. But I recommend asking permission to be on the safe side.

- If you are feeling a lot of emotion about the person/animal you would like to do surrogate tapping for, it is best to do your own tapping about that person/animal first. Our own feelings can contaminate the energy field, and if this happens the work won't be as effective. For example, if you want to tap for your

175

parent who is in a lot of physical pain, your own feelings about that parent may be consuming the attention. First tap on your own feelings about that parent, and then tap for their well-being.

- Surrogate tapping is sacred and must have the intention for the highest healing of the recipient. It is not to be used for manipulation or personal gain. For example, it is best not to tap on your partner so they stop playing video games and do the dang dishes already.

- You can do this on your own, but it is best to work with a certified practitioner.

Group Tapping

Even though working one-on-one with a practitioner is the most effective way to get results with EFT, tapping in groups is usually much more affordable, creates community, and allows for deep connection with self and others. There is something very special about tapping together in a group, and sometimes it is nice to have a reminder that you are not alone. Once upon a time, I led a morning tapping group (maybe again someday) and many blessings came from it such as community, connection and lifelong friendships.

There is a phenomenon in the EFT world called *Borrowing Benefits,* and this is available to us when we tap with a group of other people. For example, if I am participating in a tap group and we are tapping on financial stress, and I don't happen to feel any financial stress that day, I can actually still borrow benefits if I have stress from my relationship, or my health, or have a deadline of some kind. You can borrow the group benefits by simply thinking about your personal issue in your mind's eye but still follow along with the group tap. This works the other way around as well. If one person shares their feelings, and the group is tapping specifically for them, that person is actually riding on the wings of group energy, and has a whole crew of people surrogate tapping for them. Group tapping can be a wonderful option to find more tapping friends!

In summary, tapping therapy work can come in all shapes and sizes. I invite you to be open-minded about how tapping may be utilized for your lifestyle. If you have children or animals in your life, try tapping with them and see how it goes. And if you are looking for an EFT community, find a group near you or online.

15: More Tools For Taking Care Of Your Energy

*"You have everything you need for complete peace
and total happiness right now."*

—Wayne Dyer

Sensitive people are affected by their environment whether they like it or not. You cannot have too many tools to help protect your energy and keep it clean and clear. In this chapter I will share with you some practices I use for myself and have shared with my clients to help nourish your energetic space like your physical space in the home, nourishing the body with clean food and water, visualization tools, preparing for a good night's sleep, and even keeping a clean space for your money.

If you get a new house plant and it starts to wilt and turn yellow, you do not yell and scream at the plant, assuming that it is not doing enough. You start to think critically and ponder how to improve the environment for the plant to feel better and thrive. You might wonder if this plant is getting enough sunlight, was it is watered too much or too little, and is the size of the pot it lives in appropriate for its size? Does it even like this room? I was given the most adorable little plant pot, and I wasn't sure what to do with it. All of my plants were just too big for it, so I went down to the local nursery looking for a mini plant to put in it. I asked the knowledgeable lady who was working there if she could recommend a tiny plant that would be happy in this little pot. She said that yes they had some mini plants, but the thing is . . . healthy things grow.

Healthy things grow. What once fit you, may not fit you anymore, because you are growing, and evolving, and that is a good thing. Do not try to fit yourself in the same old container that you have been in for a long while. Small plant pots are adorable, but they are not meant for long-term living. The essence of this sweet life is growth, so let us create an environment for optimal growth, with plenty of room to dig your roots in deep and reach your branches up as tall as you desire.

Some of these may be fairly obvious if you have been practicing self-care for a while, and these ideas may be life-changing if they are brand new to you. But the review is always important as sometimes we know what is good for us, but have a hard time sticking to the daily practice. If you do try on some of these ideas for yourself, I bet you will be delighted to feel your energy lighter, more secure and stable, protected, and experience more freedom to be your unique sensitive self and shine bright. Everything is energy, and cleaning up our energetic space is vital to the sensitive person because something may be leaching your energy from one of these areas that you are unaware of. These practices may not be a one-and-done situation; I suggest committing to refreshing these areas of life every three to four months to maintain energy hygiene.

Clearing Physical Space

In the words of Marie Kondo, letting go is even more important than adding. Keeping your physical space clear of clutter can be life-changing for a *sensitive superhero*. Look around you right now; what do you see in your space? Ask yourself if what you see is distracting for you, nagging at you, or overwhelming you. If your home environment is not restorative, it will be very difficult to get refreshed in your downtime. To set yourself up for success, get rid of stuff you no longer need. Give away clothes you no longer wear and give away stuff that is not a part of your life vision moving forward. Our stuff has energy, and if it is not supportive energy, it is best to let it go, or at least rearrange it so it is not distracting or overwhelming you anymore.

For example, consider your sleep space; is there a screen of some kind staring at you? It can be hard to relax if a pile of paperwork or a project you haven't finished is present. Your sleep space is sacred and needs to be treated as such. Make sure you limit electronics and artificial light in this space as much as possible. If you charge your phone at night or use your phone alarm to wake up in the morning, it can be easy to be sucked into playing on your phone before bed and first thing in the morning. You know how it goes: *"Oh let me just check my Instagram, Facebook, email, bank account, and TikTok real quick before bed."* Not that it is a bad thing to be dreaming about the last kitten video that you saw, but our dream world is very much affected by what we take in during the day, especially at night. Try charging your phone at night in another room, close enough that you can hear your alarm, but far enough away that you are not tempted to grab it and scroll.

You can raise the vibration of your physical space with other tools as well:

- Smudge your living space with sage, palo santo, or a high-vibe room spray such as rose water.

- Diffuse essential oils you enjoy. This can clear the space in a room and make it smell yummy too. Essential oils carry intention. Try some that you are naturally drawn to, and thank that plant medicine for bringing its gifts into your space.

- Play some high-vibe music that makes you dance, smile, or induces relaxation.

- Clean, clean, clean your space. There is nothing like coming home to a fresh, clean, home. It feels restorative and leads to less stress as there is no other thing *to do* when you get home.

- Discard anything that you have not enjoyed for two years—letting go of the old creates more space for new blessings to arrive.

If letting go of stuff is difficult for you, I recommend tapping on the resistance aspect of this; it might give you some good insight into why it is hard to let go. Also if you have trouble sleeping at night in general, due to your environment or not, I recommend doing a few rounds of gentle tapping on the aspects of your day, or anything on your mind, that can help release the day so that you can sleep peacefully.

Eat Nutritious Foods That Your Body Loves

If you are truly sensitive, you may notice that you are also sensitive to the food and substances you put in and on your body. Be sure to eat foods that make you feel nourished and are also pleasurable to consume. We already have toxins in our air, our water, in our cleaning products, and in our pharmaceutical medicines; we do not need them in our food or beauty products as well. Eating organic fresh food is the best way to start weeding out the toxins in our lives. Pay attention to how you feel after eating certain foods, and pay attention to what you are naturally drawn to at the grocery store. Mindfully eat and chew your food. You are intuitive and your intuition will help show you the way. You can even close your eyes down and ask your body and intuition to help you by asking, "What food will deeply nourish me today? What is it that my body, mind and spirit really want?" And then listen. I would also like to add that it is beneficial to only wear clothes that your body loves, and use products that your body feels nourished by. Life is simply too short to compromise on this.

Your body is your home in this lifetime; let us care for it as much as possible.

Exercise

Move your body every day in ways that feel supportive and bring you joy. No matter your body type or ability level, there are creative ways to get moving. Exercising for at least thirty minutes a day can not only bring vitality and health, but it can also help us shake off the stress of the day, other people's opinions and energy, and get stuck energy out of your system. Essentially tapping reenacts the "shake-it-off" process, and exercise can provide a similar effect. This is why we feel so good after a workout or a tap session. Start where you are and enroll support. You are worth this time. Even if you start with dancing in your living room for three minutes a day, move that body!

Water & Hydration

Everything in the body works better when we are well hydrated. Up to 60 percent of the human body is composed of water. From our skin, to our bones, to our brains, to our hearts, lungs, and kidneys, water connects everything and increases the healthy flow of life force energy. When using our fingers to tap on the body's meridian lines, we are supporting the energetic flow, and hydration greatly helps this process.

Any time I do not feel good, I have to ask myself if I have had enough water that day, and the answer is usually no. Our bodies are water, and our bodies are cleansed with water on the inside, and on the outside. According to Dr. Emoto's book *Hidden Messages in Water,* he teaches us that we can also charge our water with positive words, so much so that it changes the molecular structure of the water. Go buy yourself a beautiful water bottle, something you really love, and put some positive words on the water bottle. You can simply write them on paper and tape them to the water bottle or find some beautiful positive message stickers online.

Social Cleanse

Sometimes being around a lot of people can drain the energy of a *sensitive superhero,* especially if we do not give ourselves the gift of recovery time. Create space in your calendar to recoup and replenish after you have a planned big day, big week, or big month. It is also beneficial to clean up your friends list by way of saying *"NO"* to social engagements that you are not truly excited about and creating distance between yourself and those you do not feel nourished by. You are allowed to be picky about who you let into your life and spend your precious time with. And if you make self-care or downtime appointments with yourself, keep them! Your appointments for yourself are just as important as any other appointment.

Healthy Boundaries

When we make a firm decision to have a boundary for whatever reason, time for self-care, time to write your book, this is the time when things/people/events start to pop out of the woodwork to challenge this boundary. So even though it is hard, I would argue that this is the most important time to hold your ground.

Boundaries are good for everyone, especially when they are clear, kind, and unapologetic. If you are afraid to hurt someone's feelings by holding a boundary, this is a great opportunity to pause, notice, and learn about yourself in the moment. Ask yourself, where is this fear coming from? What am I afraid to lose? I would also like you to consider that holding your ground could be the most loving thing you can possibly do. Have you ever said yes to something with hesitation to only then be mad at yourself for saying yes or feel resentment for the other person for asking in the first place?

For some of us, especially the recovering people pleaser, that can be the hardest shift to make. There is usually a deep fear underneath the surface that does not want to be ostracized from the group, that needs to be loved, and needs others to be OK in order to be OK ourselves. But this is the ultimate abandonment of ourselves and leads to the inevitable *"give, give, give"* and blocks the space for us to receive. For some of us, this is so ingrained that we do not realize what is happening until it is too late; you are stuck at the school board meeting again and have just volunteered to be in charge of the fall festival once more. Just like our breath, we can not only breathe in or only breathe out, but we also find the healthy balance of giving and receiving. This is best for all involved if we really give authentically and not out of a place of obligation.

Clean Up Your Money Energy

Denise Duffield-Thomas is the author of the book *Get Rich Lucky Bitch* and is a big fan of tapping. She instructs her followers to make upgrades to their money energy by buying a new fancy wallet, and have a place we are excited to keep our money in. Suze Orman, another financial guru, says to arrange the dollar bills in our wallets to all face the same direction and be right-side up. Having bills crumpled and shoved into pockets is a sign of disrespect to our money. Take the time to clean up your money energy by organizing your paperwork, receipts, bills, and so on. When we are organized, and everything looks clean and tidy, it is easier for us to receive more money energy. When our money energy is chaotic, it's not an inviting space, and hard to tell what is coming and going.

The Magic Bubble

One way to put up a metaphorical protective shield around you is to use the Magic Bubble technique. The Magic Bubble originated from the talented Matrix Reimprinting practitioner and trainer Sasha Allenby. By doing some tapping work on our younger self that experienced the trauma, decided on the limiting belief, or is stuck in a trauma capsule, we are able to go into that memory and help them. The story about my younger self creating a money belief in chapter 10 is an example of Matrix Reimprinting / Hacking Reality. Our younger self can feel safe when they have a protective bubble around them, and we can use this bubble at any time and anywhere in our current life as an adult. Good things can come into the bubble, but bad things cannot. This allows us to give and receive love from others in a safe way. You can install and reinstall the bubble if it starts to weaken. The installation button is on the chest. Put two fingers on your chest (right or left hand, it does not matter) and press on the center of the chest as if you are pressing a button in an elevator. When you press, speak out loud (or silently to yourself) "Install" and imagine the protective bubble forming around you. You can get playful with this in your imagination by deciding what color or texture you would like to make your magic bubble. This is a way to protect your auric field and give yourself the protective space that you need.

Ask for Help

Sensitive people thrive when they have support around them, the right coaching, and trusted guidance. If you are sensitive and struggling, please reach out for help. Asking for help is a super-power, and is sometimes harder than it sounds. It is not a sign of weakness, but of strength. Ask yourself, what would feel really supportive to me? It is first important to consider this, so you are able to ask clearly and specifically. Having a counselor, a coach, or a spiritual community could set you up to absolutely flourish being beautiful *you*.

Daily Spiritual Practice

Take time in the morning or throughout the day to get grounded in a daily spiritual practice designed especially for you. Having a small daily practice can bring you back to yourself, when life pulls us away. Pick one (or a few) small practice(s), decide how long you will dedicate to that practice, and build from there. If the goal is too big, it will be more difficult to stick to. For the longest time, I had the goal to meditate for twenty minutes a day. I tried to accomplish this for three years, and maybe did it a handful of times. When I changed the goal to five minutes a day, before I knew it I had meditated every day for a whole month. Remember it is a *practice*, not a *perfect*. Here is a list of ideas to get the wheels turning for your own practice, which you can design for yourself.

1. Meditate for 5–10 minutes a day.

2. Dance in the living room for 3–5 minutes a day.

3. Gratitude journal for 10 minutes a day.

4. Tap for 10 minutes a day.

5. Stretch for 5–10 minutes a day.

6. Walk for 10 minutes a day.

7. Do a 30–60-minute yoga class online or in a studio.

8. Visualize what you want for 5 minutes a day.

I made this daily practice sheet that I use for myself, and you can try it as a free download on my website.

DAILY DOSE
OF PEACEFUL PRACTICES

MY AWESOME THEME FOR
THE WEEK:

M   T   W   T   F   S   S

_____ ◯ ◯ ◯ ◯ ◯ ◯ ◯

_____ ◯ ◯ ◯ ◯ ◯ ◯ ◯

_____ ◯ ◯ ◯ ◯ ◯ ◯ ◯

_____ ◯ ◯ ◯ ◯ ◯ ◯ ◯

_____ ◯ ◯ ◯ ◯ ◯ ◯ ◯

_____ ◯ ◯ ◯ ◯ ◯ ◯ ◯

MY SELF-CARE TIME IS
PRECIOUS TO ME BECAUSE:

NOTES TO MYSELF:

Get Back on Track

No matter how prepared, organized, and collected we might feel, unexpected events in life can throw us off our center in a blink of an eye. Avoiding this is not really an option; life happening is just a part of life. Oftentimes it happens all at once too; I know that you know. Have you ever had your car break down, get dumped by someone you were really excited about, and find out you had your identity stolen in the same week? Just me? These events are inevitable and can even be considered an opportunity when we dig deep and pull ourselves up again after we have been knocked down.

Game plan for how to pick yourself up again when life knocks us down:

1. Timeline: Do not put pressure on yourself for a timeline to get back up again. We are all built wildly differently, and we do not all operate on the same timeline. Without pressure, allow yourself a certain amount of time to wallow: one hour, one day, one week, and so on. Pick a day for when you will come back online. You can even write on your calendar, "Lisa is back!"

2. Self-Care: What has you feeling like yourself again? Maybe it is as simple as taking a nap or scheduling a massage or self-care.

3. Reframe: Life is happening for you, not to you. My favorite astrologer, Kacy Dane, taught me about how Mercury retrograde gets a bad rap. I am sure you have heard before not to make travel plans, sign contracts, or start a new project during Mercury retrograde. But what is really happening with the technical issues, the interruptions, and so on is a course correction. Things get messed up slightly now,

189

so that they may be corrected, upgraded, and run smoother in the future. Mess-ups happen as a gift, if we can see it that way, so things will be more efficient down the line.

The Circle of White Light

When I was a kid, the most important thing in the world to me was making my free-throw shots in my basketball game. It may sound silly now, but it was ingrained in me that free throws are absolutely what win games. And when it was my turn to shoot, I better sink that shot. I would always get nervous . . . I would feel the pressure. And then I heard something that helped me step into my power, and it extended way beyond the basketball court. In Dennis Waitley's book *The Psychology of Winning*, he teaches about stepping into your most powerful self by seeing a circle of white light on the floor, a few feet away from you. Imagine it glowing with vibrancy and clarity. Know that when you decide to step into this circle, you are stepping into your most powerful, confident, skilled self in that moment, and you can be in that space for the day. I would see this circle on the free-throw line on the basketball court, and step into it as I approached the line with the basketball in my hands. And guess what? I started making more free throws.

I hope you continue to create space for yourself to thrive and are able to use some of these ideas to keep your energy clean and clear for optimal thriving as a *sensitive superhero.*

Conclusion

"There is always light. If only we are brave enough to see it,
if only we are brave enough to be it."

—Amanda Gorman

If you are one of my sensitive sisters or brothers, my deepest desire for you is to feel safe in your skin, own your unique beauty, and thrive while sharing that beauty bravely with the world. You are more powerful, capable, and important to the collective than you will ever know. We need you well and good, and shining bright like a diamond. You deserve to feel good being your *sensitive superhero* self, tears and all.

My sincere hope is that you feel inspired after reading the stories in this book. My deepest desire is that you know that there is nothing wrong with you and that you are an important gift to the world. Hopefully, EFT tapping can help you keep your emotional freedom garden watered, pruned, and groomed so that you can share your unique gifts fully with the world. I hope you have grasped by now that the key to not crying is in fact to allow the tears to flow. It is important to let them move through you in a way that is safe for you. By allowing yourself to get out all of the gunk below the surface, you won't need to fight against yourself anymore. Now you will be able to use your precious energy for your craft, for your relationships, and of course, for yourself.

I want you to start tapping, even if you are fumbling, even if you are not doing it perfectly; I want you to give it the old college try. If you lack confidence, remember that confidence comes from action. Go for it! I would like you to tap by yourself, tap with a group, tap with a professional practitioner, and tap along with videos. My wish for you is to feel all of those things you feel so deeply, let the tears come in a safe way, and let those emotions be transformed and transmuted into something positive instead of taking up real estate in your mind or holding space in your body. All of the self-help tools in the world are helpful ideally, but they are useless if we do not actually use them. It is time for you to move forward in your life, not FEAR-ward.

A dear friend of mine grows flowers in her garden and then photographs them when they bloom. She finds dahlia flowers in her garden that are literally bigger than her head, and she is able to capture their beauty, uniqueness, and dare I say sexiness, in a picture. One day we were talking about love and loss, and the different events that happen to us throughout our lives that we never saw coming. For example, the loss of a parent, a health crisis, or going through a breakup after twenty-five years together, and we are somehow just supposed to know how to put ourselves back together and be OK after these events.

Humans are miraculously resilient. If you think about it, it is pretty incredible that we are all still walking around with all of the trauma, adversity, and heartache we have been through. Even with all of the crappy parts of life, things do seem to turn out OK, even though it does not feel that way when we are in the middle of it. But maybe, we are going to be OK, because that is our inherent design. The best nutrients in the garden actually come from the fertilizer. So maybe the "crap" of life actually ends up enriching our lives, shaping us, and giving us a whole lot of character. We get through it because we are nature too, that regenerates and has its cycles and seasons.

As we sat in my friend's garden, she held out her hand to show me some anemone corms. She had me examine them, what looked like little brown clumps of dirt. She went on to tell me that if you were to cut them in half, they look like raw potato nothingness. But when you plant them in the dirt, they grow into stunning, vibrantly colored flowers, just being their beautiful selves, as if they were encoded to be that way. My wish for you is that you know that the beauty of who you are, including your sensitivity, is deeply encoded into your being by perfect design. There has not been a mistake; you are encoded, just like these anemone corms, to be your unapologetically brilliant and gifted self. In fact, nothing can take away from the beauty of who you are.

Thank you for coming on this journey with me to learn this tool of EFT tapping. I sincerely hope that it can serve you and the *sensitive superheroes* in your life. And if you do still cry, even after tapping, I hope that you don't apologize for it, but know you are giving yourself good medicine for the spirit, as no pill or prescription can give you what your healing tears can give you. EFT has essentially helped me in every area of my life, and this is why I am so honored to share it with you.

Resources

Books:

Hacking Reality
by Rob Nelson

The Science Behind Tapping
by Peta Stapleton, Ph. D.

The Highly Sensitive Person
by Elaine N. Aron

You Can Heal Your Life
by Louise Hay

Transform Your Beliefs, Transform Your Life
by Karl Dawson & Kate Marillat

8 Keys to Brain Body Balance
by Robert Scaer

The Biology of Belief
by Bruce Lipton

YouTube:

Tapping with Steph (my channel)

Brad Yates

Margarate Lynch

Finding an EFT Practitioner:

Certified EFT Practitioner Directories

tappingthematrixacademy.com/eft-practitioner-directory

thetappingsolution.com/eft-practitioners

Low-cost EFT Clinic:

tappingthematrixacademy.com/academy-clinic

Acknowledgments

To my parents, Donald Dodds, Meladee McCarty, and Hanoch McCarty, and to my whole family, "Thank you" just doesn't cut it. My gratitude for you and your continuous support, playfulness, and generosity expands beyond words I can express.

To my clients and students, it is my honor and privilege to work with you and be a sacred mirror for you. Thank you for choosing me as a guide and allowing me to share your stories.

To my EFT mentor and friend Rob Nelson, thank you for teaching me all that you know about EFT and Matrix Reimprinting / Hacking Reality. Your unwavering support and guidance have been an incredible blessing in my life.

To my soul sisters, thank you for witnessing my tears, for your fierce love and friendship, and for your prayers. The world needs your light, and I am so grateful to walk beside you on this path.

To Biffy Fox Cotter, thank you for reminding me to never dim my light, but to shine bright and let Spirit work through me now and always.

To Monica Allred Biery, thank you for making me a *book-writing-retreat* care package and for the hundreds of texts encouraging me through the process of birthing this book. You are my coolest friend.

To my EFT buddies Deanna Lyons and Victoria Vines, thank you for inspiring me endlessly, tapping with me, and most of all, for your friendship. You are a bright light in this world.

To my writing buddies in the Sexy Writers Club, you are pure gold, and I am so grateful to cocreate with you.

To Kelsen, thank you for reminding me to dream big and that anything is possible.

To Alcy, thank you for being someone I can trust and confide in, all while being a creative genius.

To Jenna Dennis, thank you for helping me bring this book's qi vibration into harmony, sessions with you are my absolute favorite.

To my book coach and friend Cynthia Gregory (from Mayacamas Press), thank you for being my book Sherpa and getting me to the finish line; I truly could not have completed this labor of love without you.

To Mother Earth and my garden, thank you for your teaching every day. May we all listen deeper and more often to your wisdom.

About the Author

Founder of the Emotional Freedom Academy and EFT tapping superstar, Steph Dodds is a healer who loves answering the hollers of her heart and supports others in doing the same. Steph has authored three EFT tap-a-long courses, including one for the DailyOM, From Heartbreak to Soulmate with the Magic of Tapping.

Steph is a heart-centered sensitive soul and enjoys working with clients one-on-one in her private EFT Tapping & Matrix Reimprinting / Hacking Reality practice. She brings a sense of humor and lightheartedness to this deep soul work, as well as her fifteen years in the wellness industry adding her nutrition knowledge, restorative yoga principles, and shamanic energy healing to her clients. EFT tapping has profoundly upgraded her life experience and that is why she is so passionate about sharing this self-soothing, stress-relief tool and education with others. Steph also leads trainings for people who would like to become EFT practitioners and offers FREE tapping videos on her YouTube channel, "Tapping with Steph."

Founding member of the Sexy Writer's Club, Steph leads groups of tapping for creative expression so that others can let their true passions shine and share their gifts with the world.

You can find Steph teaching herself how to garden, dancing in her living room, walking around Sacramento, California, looking for fresh local organic food, spending yoga weekends with her soul sisters, and saying hello to every dog she meets.

Connect with Steph

stephdodds.tapwithsteph.com

www.youtube.com/c/TappingwithSteph

www.instagram.com/emotionalfreedomacademy

www.linkedin.com/in/stephdodds

www.facebook.com/emotionalfreedomacademy

www.ingramcontent.com/pod-product-compliance
Lightning Source LLC
Chambersburg PA
CBHW060504130626
46553CB00002B/405